I FORGIVE YOU

Choosing Freedom Over Bondage

DONNA D. FERGUSON, PhD, LPC

MW01485311

I FORGIVE YOU: Choosing Freedom Over Bondage

ISBN: 979-8-9872196-9-0

Copyright © 2023 by Donna D. Ferguson, PhD, LPC

All rights reserved. No part of this publication may be reproduced, distributed, or transmitted in any form or by any means, including photocopying, recording, or other electronic or mechanical methods, without the prior written permission of the publisher, except in the case of brief quotations embodied in critical reviews and certain other noncommercial uses permitted by copyright law. All scripture references are from the King James Version. For permission requests, write to the publisher, addressed "Attention: Permissions Coordinator," at the address below.

Published by: Concise Publishing
2474 Walnut St. #105
Cary, NC 27518
www.ConcisePublishing.us

To my dear husband, Marcus, whose unwavering belief in me and my potential continues to be the bedrock upon which I stand. Your encouragement empowers me to embrace my true self and achieve my highest aspirations. To you, I owe a gratitude that words can not express.

To my sons, Brandon and Marcus, who inspire me every day to trust in who I am and the unique essence I carry into this world. Your life expressions encourage me to believe in the power of my own voice and the strength of my convictions.

TO THE READER

I Forgive You: Choosing Freedom Over Bondage is intended for anyone who has ever been hurt and found it challenging to embark on the journey called forgiveness. If you've ever felt weighed down by resentment, anger, or pain resulting from others' actions or even your own, this work was designed and will speak directly to you. It delves into the complex emotional landscape of hurt and forgiveness, offering insights, understanding, and a pathway forward. Forgiveness is a choice, but the choice to forgive or not to forgive has consequences. I hope that by the time you finish reading you will have chosen freedom because to choose not to forgive is psychological and emotional bondage. Also, if you choose to dismiss the process of healing from unforgiveness, understand that it doesn't go away over time. A choice to avoid the process is still a decision and no decision is still a decision made.

Here is why I sincerely believe that you should read *I Forgive You: Choosing Freedom Over Bondage* and commit to doing the work of forgiving both yourself and others in your life:

a. **Universal Experience of Hurt-** It is important to understand that hurt is a universal human experience. Everyone, at some point in their life, feels or has felt wronged or betrayed. This work acknowledges the varied, often difficult emotions that accompany such experiences. It speaks to the shared human condition of pain and the universal need for healing and understanding, providing a sense of solidarity and recognition of your feelings. I promise you are not alone nor do you have to walk it alone.

b. **Understanding the Nature of Forgiveness-** Forgiveness is more times than not, misunderstood. We often think forgiveness means to condone the pain and forget the impact of the pain, which often leads to building a wall to protect from the experience and future pain. This is not the true essence of forgiveness but often what we do to survive. This writing clarifies what forgiveness truly entails — it is a personal act of freedom and liberation, a release from the emotional burden of the pain experienced and the past. By reading this, I believe you will gain a deeper understanding of forgiveness, empowering you to make informed and conscious choices about your emotional well-being. *You'll never conquer what you won't confront.*

c. **Empowering Choice-** Choosing to forgive is an act of empowerment all by itself, it's more about your will and not singularly your mind and emotions. This work emphasizes the power and authority you hold in the process of forgiveness. It highlights that while the journey may be challenging, it is also incredibly rewarding. By engaging with this work, you are taking a step towards reclaiming control over your emotional life, moving beyond victimhood to a position of strength and resilience.

d. **Healing and Growth-** Forgiveness is integral to your healing and personal growth. Holding on to hurt and anger can stunt your emotional and psychological development and affect your overall quality of life. This writing provides perspectives and strategies for healing through forgiveness, highlighting how letting go of resentment which is a byproduct of unforgiveness can lead to increased peace, improved relationships, and a more optimistic outlook on life. Did you know that unforgiveness has a way of stifling your creativity? It absolutely impacts all that you are.

e. **Compassionate and Caring Approach-** This work is crafted with compassion and care, recognizing the delicate nature of hurt and forgiveness. It approaches the subject with empathy, offering support and understanding to those struggling with these difficult emotions. It is a supportive guide designed to help you navigate through the pain toward a place of healing and peace. Your health and healing are more important to me than you can imagine. I want to help heal the world, one mind at a time. Imagine a mentally healthy world. Just imagine for a moment your life without the pain of unforgiveness. How would your life be different?

f. **Encouragement for Self-Forgiveness-** Just as important as forgiving others is forgiving oneself. This work delves into the critical role of self-forgiveness in the healing process. It addresses the feelings of guilt, shame, and self-blame that can accompany mistakes and failures, offering a path towards self-compassion and forgiveness.

Again, I believe that *I Forgive You: Choosing Freedom Over Bondage* is for you if you've ever felt stuck in a cycle of unforgiveness, if you've struggled with the weight of past hurts, or if you simply seek a deeper understanding of how to move forward emotionally. By reading and engaging with the insights and guidance offered, you'll be equipped to do the work of forgiving — a work that, while challenging, has the potential to transform your life, freeing you from the bonds of the past and opening you up to a future of emotional freedom and peace.

TABLE OF CONTENTS

INTRODUCTION

Forgiveness is often seen as a complex emotional and psychological journey, deeply intertwined with our experiences of hurt, pain, and betrayal. At its core, forgiveness is about a choice — a powerful, personal decision that each individual faces in the aftermath of hurt. This choice is not just about the other person or the relationship, but also significantly about one's own mental and emotional well-being. The path to forgiveness or unforgiveness stems from the deep-seated psychological and emotional pain caused by intentional or perceived wrongs, and the choice made in response to this pain has profound implications.

Everyone, at some point, experiences hurt inflicted by others, whether through betrayal, rejection, injustice, or misunderstanding. This hurt can cut deeply, affecting not just our emotions but our perceptions of self, others, and the world around us. The psychological and emotional pain that ensues can leave lasting scars, influencing behavior, relationships, and overall mental health. The nature and intensity of this pain are deeply personal, colored by individual experiences, values, and vulnerabilities.

In the wake of hurt, individuals stand at a crossroads between forgiveness and unforgiveness. This choice is influenced by a myriad of factors including personal beliefs, cultural background, the nature of the hurt, and the individual's emotional resilience and psychological state.

One of the most profound and challenging steps we can undertake is the choice or act of forgiveness. When you embark at the crossroads of deciding to forgive or not to forgive, understand that your choice is not a fleeting moment of compassion; it is a powerful and transformative process that impacts your mental, emotional, and physical well-being. It involves acknowledging hurt and pain, releasing resentment, and ultimately, finding a path forward that is not weighed down by the burdens of the past.

The idea that forgiveness is a sign of weakness or an act of condoning hurtful behavior is a misconception. In reality, forgiveness is a testament to one's strength and resilience. Yes, it is about releasing someone from their responsibility, and it is also about reclaiming control from those who have wronged us and refusing to let their actions dictate our peace and happiness. At the crossroads of the decision to forgive or not to forgive, is seldom easy but it is worth it. It is filled with emotional complexity and requires a deep understanding of its nature, causes, and the profound impact unforgiveness can have on our lives. It is a choice. The choice is easy, but can also be difficult but worth doing the work to be healed.

Choosing **Forgiveness** is essentially choosing to release the resentment, anger, and desire for retribution that binds us to the person who has caused the hurt. It is a decision to let go of the negative emotions and thoughts that consume our mental and emotional energy. Forgiveness does not necessarily mean forgetting or reconciling with the offender; rather, it is about freeing oneself from the emotional shackles of the past. It is a choice that leads to mental and emotional freedom, opening up space for healing, growth, and peace.

On the other hand, choosing **Unforgiveness** - not to forgive - or being unable to forgive due to the depth of the hurt - can lead to a state of unforgiveness, where anger, resentment, and bitterness continue to fester. This emotional bondage can become a heavy burden, affecting mental health, relationships, and even physical well-being. It is a state that keeps individuals tied to the past, to the hurt, and to the person who caused it (the offender). Yes, I referenced the person as an offender because you will never have unforgiveness without first having an offense. The person responsible for executing the hurt is an offender.

FURTHER UNDERSTANDING OF THE IMPLICATIONS OF THE CHOICE.

I know we have only mentioned the offender or the person that caused you harm briefly thus far and that is intentional because I do not want to give them any additional power.

I do not want to make them the focus of your healing as this is about you and your choices. Taking the focus from the one who caused your pain, begins the process of lessening their power. I also understand how hard it can be to deal with the pain because it can feel as though it is happening to you freshly over and over. Many will hide their wounds with hopes of never having to deal with the pain or hope that time will heal the wound. It is only natural to do this as no one ever tells us how to process our pain; however, we're often taught how to hide or detach from it. We often remain stuck because of the pain but it's important to understand that pain in healing and recovery is natural. There is a pain in forgiveness recovery and being able to say *I Forgive You* is an essential part of the healing and recovery process. Providing the framework for your healing and recovery or laying out the case, will help you more easily to make an informed decision and begin to heal. No one can make the decision for you, it is something you must choose; however, I can provide the tools to support your decision. Some will find it difficult to make a decision to heal or not to heal but understand that "no decision is still a decision made.

Again, the choice between forgiveness and unforgiveness carries significant implications. Though it has potentially been hard to let go and you may be rationalizing or fighting with such thoughts as:

a. What about my offender or the person who hurt me?
b. What about what they did to me?
c. They don't deserve to be forgiven.
d. They hurt me so bad.
e. It seems like they don't care about what they did.
f. What's their punishment?
g. They win if I let it go?
h. This might be too hard for me to work through.

Know that *ALL* of your thoughts and questions are normal, in fact, your thoughts and emotions are expected because they are normal reactions to an abnormal experience. You <u>are not</u> abnormal; the experience or trauma is abnormal. We were not designed to cause or experience pain as it is traumatic to our psyche and emotions but there are answers to the healing of the pain when it occurs- we simply have to be willing to go through the process. Therefore, again, if you do not process through your pain, the outcome is a potentially unrealized abnormal mental and emotional state. Whatever you don't deal with or process through well, will always inform your future.

The following chapters are not merely about the immediate emotional relief or burden that we often try to manage, get over, or hide; it's about the long-term effects on one's life and health- Mental and Emotional Freedom. Choosing forgiveness can lead to profound mental and emotional freedom or liberation. Unforgiveness is associated with lower levels of depression, anxiety, and anger, as well as overall satisfaction with life. Forgiveness can enhance psychological resilience, leading to better coping skills and a more optimistic outlook on life.

If you choose otherwise- conversely, unforgiveness can lead to emotional bondage, where the individual remains trapped in a cycle of negative emotions and memories. This state is linked to higher instances of mental health issues, poorer physical health, and reduced overall well-being. It can strain or break relationships, lead to a pessimistic outlook on life, and hinder personal growth, maturity, and happiness. Unforgiveness can become a clinical issue.

This journey is about restoration; the healing of your SOUL (Thoughts, will, and emotions). I have not found anyone who truly chose to forgive, regret their decision. However, it is important to also understand that everyone is not ready to forgive right away, forgiveness forced or done prematurely could lead to dissatisfaction; thus, why I am laying out the case. You get to decide "When". If you begin to read and you are not quite ready, be okay with putting it down, just do not forget to build a plan to pick it up and start again. Your healing is necessary for the restoration of your joy, peace, and longevity.

You also do not have to do this work alone. Some forms of hurt you can work through on your own, some forms may require a friend or family member with wisdom, and in some cases, you may need a Mental Health Professional. If you desire to do the work, but do not feel comfortable doing it alone, I encourage you to find a Licensed Professional Mental Health Clinician who can support and help you.

** DISCLAIMER- You will hear me repeat certain emotions, topics, and phrases throughout. By being repetitive and reinforcing new knowledge, it will help you learn, process, and heal. Also, some emotions will need to be dealt with on different levels **

ARE YOU READY? LET'S DO THIS.

Of course, I am going to always recommend our Licensed Professional Mental Health Professionals (LPCs/LMHCs) as they are amazing at this work and more than qualified and equipped to help you.

CHAPTER 1

FORGIVENESS: A MULTIFACETED PROCESS

Forgiveness is a deeply personal, yet universally understood concept. It involves a conscious decision to release feelings of resentment or vengeance toward a person or group who has harmed you, regardless of whether they deserve your forgiveness or not. It is important to note that forgiving someone does not mean justifying or excusing their wrongdoing. Instead, it is about freeing yourself from the burden of continuous emotional and psychological pain, and the behaviors such as anger and bitterness. Forgiveness is a journey that varies greatly from one individual to another. For some, it may be swift and uncomplicated, while for others, it might be a long and turbulent path marked by emotional introspection and gradual acceptance. Despite the wide range, forgiveness can be accomplished. It begins with deciding; and choosing to forgive.

Forgiveness, by definition, is an act of pardoning someone for an offense or mistake, is a deeply personal and often challenging decision, reflecting a deliberate choice to release feelings of resentment and thoughts of revenge. This act of pardoning, whether the hurt was intentional or the result of a mistake, involves a conscious shift in perspective and emotion, steering away from harboring negative feelings that ultimately serve to prolong one's own suffering.

When the offense is intentional, the act of forgiving can be particularly difficult. It requires a person to look beyond the deliberate harm inflicted by another and to make a conscious choice not to let that action continue to dictate their emotional state. The decision to forgive in such cases is not a validation of the act nor a sign of weakness; rather, it is an empowering step that frees the individual from the toxic, ongoing cycle of anger and resentment. It allows the recipient of the offense or hurt to reclaim their peace and move forward, even when the other party may not have expressed remorse or even want to. Forgiveness in this context is less about the offender and more about the forgiver's well-being and release from the emotional bondage that unforgiveness perpetuates.

In instances where the hurt is the result of a mistake or negligence, forgiveness might be easier to extend, but is no less significant. Recognizing the fallibility of human nature, including our own, can pave the way for empathy and understanding. Everyone makes mistakes, and often, these are not intended to cause the hurt that they do. By pardoning someone for a mistake, and acknowledging that everyone is capable of error, individuals foster a more compassionate and forgiving environment. This not only aids in healing personal wounds but also contributes to healthier, more understanding relationships.

Ultimately, the conscious decision to forgive and let go is a choice in favor of a person's mental and emotional health. Holding on to resentment and anger is often likened to carrying a heavy burden — it is exhausting and damaging to the self. Unforgiveness keeps individuals tethered to moments of pain, continuously inflicting emotional distress and hindering one's ability to enjoy life and engage positively with others. By choosing forgiveness, individuals free themselves from these chains. They allow themselves to heal, grow, and open up to new experiences and joys. Remember, forgiveness does not erase the past, but it ensures that the past no longer holds a detrimental grip on your present and future. It is a gift one gives to oneself, a profound act of self-care and emotional liberation.

In *The Tree Called Trauma: How to Become Unstuck from a Place Called Here*, I discuss the fruit produced by unforgiveness, an analogy that helps individuals see how hurt and pain produce behavioral outcomes that are unhealthy. Unforgiveness is in all of its ways unhealthy and can and will bear toxic fruit, manifesting as ongoing resentment, anger, and a host of other physical, psychological, emotional, and behavioral ailments and issues. Unforgiveness keeps us tied to the very incidents and individuals we most wish to be free from. In contrast, embracing forgiveness can lead us to healing and freedom. It can restore broken relationships, promote understanding and empathy, and foster a healthier, more joyful existence.

However, it is crucial to not only recognize but accept that forgiveness is a process. Not accepting it as a process that requires time, can cause harm to the one desiring to forgive. It does not happen overnight and the time it takes is dependent upon the individual. No one should be rushed to forgive despite the reason. Forgiveness needs to be handled with care and compassion. It's about gradually letting go of the grip that pain has on the heart and mind. Taking your time to process well ensures your healing and wholeness.

As we prepare to delve deeper into the multifaceted aspects of forgiveness, let us keep in mind that we aim to guide you through understanding what forgiveness truly entails, its challenges, and, most importantly, the freedom and peace it can bring into your life; one step at a time.

I know many of you may want to dive right in and get it over with but this can be dangereous if you're not ready. It's important to understand the nature of a problem before working to correct a problem. I understand it is human behavior to want to solve a problem as quickly as possible. Our greatest challenge in doing so is when we seek to solve without seeking to understand, we often cause more interrelated issues. So, right now we are seeking to understand and gain insight into the process called forgiveness.

In all our getting, let's get understanding

CHAPTER 2

FORGIVENESS AS A PROCESS: WHAT ARE THE BASIC STAGES

Forgiveness is indeed an intricate process that unfolds in layers and stages, varying greatly from one individual to another. It involves a complex interplay of emotions, memories, and personal beliefs, all of which contribute to the difficulty and duration of the forgiveness journey. The emotional complexity of this work requires courage, patience, and often a significant shift in perspective.

The process of forgiveness is emotionally complex because it involves confronting painful and often deeply buried feelings. For many, the journey begins with the raw emotions of anger, betrayal, and hurt. These feelings often validate the individual's experience and pain and are not uncommon. As the process unfolds, these intense emotions may give way to sadness, longing, or confusion, reflecting the multifaceted nature of hurt and human relationships. Forgiving someone often requires revisiting these emotions, understanding their roots, and actively working to transform them. This transformation is not linear; it can involve moving back and forth between different feelings, each layer revealing new insights and challenges. The key to emotions is not to dismiss them or regard them as right or wrong. Your emotions give you insight into what is going on in the soul of who you are. The important key to emotions is to accept that you have them and seek to understand what they are rooted in so that you can process through it. There may be layers and that's okay- the work is worth it.

The depth and longevity of the hurt can significantly impact the forgiveness process as some may struggle with the idea that they could forgive. You still can, we simply need to do the work. When the hurt has been carried for a long time or is particularly deep-seated, perhaps due to repeated offenses or profound betrayal, the emotional work required can be more substantial. Each individual's journey through these layers is unique, influenced by personal history, resilience, and the nature of the hurt itself. Some might find themselves dealing with layers of anger before they can reach the underlying hurt or betrayal. Others may need to address feelings of self-blame or shame that complicate the ability to forgive. This journey requires one to peel back these layers, often one by one, to address the full scope of their emotional pain.

For many, the inability to forgive is tied to unresolved trauma. The traumatic experience, whether related to the specific offense or past unrelated incidents can color the individual's emotional response and ability to process and release the hurt. Trauma can make the hurt feel immediate and raw, regardless of how much time has passed, and can lead to a heightened state of emotional reactivity. Addressing this trauma is often a necessary step in the forgiveness process, sometimes requiring professional help such as therapy or counseling. It involves not only acknowledging the trauma but also working through its emotional and psychological impact.

I encourage all intense and serious trauma work to be done with a professional because they can help manage your emotional pain, help you manage expectations, and help you develop intricate short-term and long-term goals that will facilitate your healing. The danger in working alone or in isolation is that sometimes we think we can do it on our own not realizing the seriousness and depth of the work that needs to be done. When you have a sprained or broken bone, you go to the doctor. If we have a high fever that we cannot bring down with basic over-the-counter medications, we go to the doctor. If you are hurting in your digestive system and cannot hold food, we go to the doctor. If your heart flutters, your blood pressure goes up, and you have headaches, you go to the doctor. Trauma is a mental medical condition that needs to be treated by the right professional who works with the mind. The misnomer is that mental health work does not require a professional, but the truth is it does. Let us not self-diagnose and become our own doctors. Your mind is precious and needs the right care (That was my soapbox moment) back to the process.

Letting go of hurt and resentment is a critical aspect of forgiveness. However, it is important to understand that this release is typically gradual and may not feel complete right away. Remember, letting go is not about forgetting the hurt or pretending it did not matter; it is about loosening its grip on your heart and mind. This part of the process is about acceptance — accepting what happened, the emotions it stirred, and the fact that the past cannot be changed. It is about making peace with the hurt enough to stop it from dictating your emotional state and choices. Letting go involves a level of submission which is another choice that has to be made in the process.

Choosing to forgive is a process that requires a certain level of submission — a willingness to engage with difficult emotions and memories, to challenge one's perspectives and reactions, and to remain open to the shifts and changes that this journey might bring. This submission is not passive; it is an active and often challenging engagement with one's inner world. It involves patience and understanding that the process cannot be rushed and that its course might be unpredictable and non-linear.

We now understand that forgiveness can and usually is a complex, deeply emotional journey that involves a multifaceted array of feelings, memories, and personal growth. It's a path that can lead to profound healing and freedom but requires intentional emotional work and patience with yourself. Each person's journey is unique, shaped by their individual experiences, strengths, and the nature of the hurt they have endured. Engaging in this process is a brave and worthwhile endeavor, offering the promise of peace, closure, and a deeper understanding of oneself and others.

"Never judge your journey by someone else's, you're unique and of high value, judging your story or journey by someone else's will cause you to devalue who you are".

Forgiveness as a process in basic terms and tenets may look like this:

1. **Acknowledgment of Hurt**: Forgiveness often starts with acknowledging the hurt and allowing oneself to feel the emotions associated with the pain. This can be the most challenging part, as it requires facing the reality of what happened and the impact it has had. In the acknowledgment phase do not make rationalization. Rationalization or justifications can cause a false sense of healing or complicate the process by causing a misalignment between the mind and the heart. Simply accept that it happens. Is it true that it occurred, yes, or no? Answering yes or no does not change what occurred, it simply says it happened. Acknowledging that it happened instead of avoiding it helps to move the process. Rationalizing does not change the

fact that it happened. Remember, hurt, disappointment, and forgiveness are universal- you are not alone, and you are not a problem, what you experienced is.

2. **Understanding and Empathy**: Part of the process involves trying to understand the circumstances or motivations behind the offense. This does not mean excusing the behavior, but rather trying to see the situation from a broader perspective, which can sometimes help in reducing the personal sting of the offense. I want to start by saying, people are imperfect, and we all have flaws. To what degree we have flaws varies based on experiences, environments, and belief systems about people, relationships, and the lens through which we view the world. Some of those systems of thinking are unhealthy and dysfunctional thus causing you and everyone around you to experience some form of hurt at least once in your lives. As you seek to understand the circumstances or motivation behind the offense, you will not always understand. It is important; however, to accept that you may not understand- this is also a choice. We'll need to spend some time here with being okay not always understanding the motives of someone else.

3. **Emotional Release**: Forgiveness involves an emotional release, letting go of the anger, resentment, or desire for revenge that might have built up. This release is often gradual and might require revisiting the hurt from different angles or at different times. The emotional release involves choosing to let go. Ask yourself the question, "Why don't I want to let go or release the person who caused me hurt?" Why am I choosing to hold on to the hurt that is not only causing me pain but will cause greater pain if I keep it" What's behind my reason to hold on?" Be honest with yourself as honesty helps you move through the

pain to recovery. Pain is a part of healing just as when you tear a muscle or break a bone and are required to attend physical therapy- and the pain in physical therapy is a sign of healing. Healing is good, but it does not always feel good early on. It is work but the goal is to stay the course.

4. **Decision to Forgive**: Eventually, forgiveness involves a conscious decision to let go of the grievances. It is an active choice, sometimes made repeatedly, to not let the hurt dictate one's emotional state or future. The decision in and of itself is a process. It is like loosening a rope. Deciding will be discussed in more detail in the next chapter.

5. **Transformation and Healing**: The final stages of forgiveness involve a transformation in feelings and attitudes toward the offender and the offense. It leads to healing, not just in the sense of moving past the hurt, but also in growing from the experience. Transformation, again in and of itself is a process. Transformation begins with renewing the mind about the circumstances and situations. Renewing the mind requires choosing a new thought, which leads to a new thought pattern, and thus a transformed mindset surrounding the issue. The brain is neuroplastic, meaning it can change. When you work at choosing to change your thinking about an issue, the more you work at it and choose the thought, it becomes a marker on your neuropathway. You create a new transformed thought pattern, not controlled by your former pain. Healing progressively takes place during the transformation.

Let's go back to making a conscious decision to forgive as it will help with the transformation and healing process.

CHAPTER 3

FORGIVENESS AS A PROCESS

Making a conscious decision to forgive is a pivotal moment in the journey through transformation, healing, and emotional freedom. This decision is far more than a momentary thought or a simple declaration; it is a deep, intentional commitment to a path that is often difficult and uncertain when you look down the road that has to be traveled. A conscious decision is a choice made with full awareness of the hurt and the complexity of the emotions involved.

Below is what making a conscious decision to forgive entails and what it looks like in practice. First, what it entails is awareness and deliberation, intentionality, and purpose, and finally, commitment to the process.

Awareness and Deliberation: Making a conscious decision means being fully aware of the hurt and the various emotions it has stirred. It involves a deliberate choice to move forward in the healing process, acknowledging the difficulty of the path ahead but choosing it, nonetheless. This awareness also includes understanding the implications of forgiveness — that it is for one's own peace and well-being and not necessarily about reconciling with or excusing the offender.

Being fully aware of the hurt and the emotions it has stirred is an essential first step in the conscious decision to forgive. This awareness involves a deep, honest exploration of how the hurt has impacted one's life, acknowledging not just the initial pain but also the lingering effects on one's emotional well-being, relationships, and self-perception. It requires confronting feelings that might be complex and contradictory — anger, sadness, betrayal, longing, and more. This awareness is crucial because it validates the individual's experience and pain, setting a foundation for genuine healing. It is about recognizing the full extent of the emotional landscape, not diminishing, or avoiding it, which allows for a more authentic and effective forgiveness process.

Choosing to move forward in the healing process, despite being fully aware of the pain and complexity of emotions, is a testament to one's courage and resilience. It means acknowledging the difficulty of the path ahead — the emotional work required, the potential for setbacks, and the need for patience and perseverance. But it also involves a recognition of the potential for healing and growth that lies beyond the hurt. Choosing to move forward is an act of hope, a belief that despite the challenges, there is a possibility for peace, understanding, and a renewed sense of self. It is a commitment to oneself, to one's future, and to the emotional freedom that forgiveness can bring.

Understanding the implications of forgiveness for one's own peace and well-being is about recognizing that forgiveness is ultimately a personal act of freedom that you choose for yourself, not dependent upon the individuals who caused you harm. It is not necessarily about reconciling with the offender or excusing their actions; it's about releasing the emotional hold that the hurt has on your life. It is at this juncture that through understanding, the focus shifts from the offender and their actions to the forgiver and their journey towards peace. This decision makes forgiveness, in this sense, a self-focused act — it's about choosing what's best for your mental and emotional health, choosing not to allow the negative emotions to remain housed in your heart, mind, and thus your body (yes, your body) but choosing to open up space for more positive emotions and experiences. Who wouldn't want positive emotions over negative emotions, when you have the power to choose?

Question: What would make someone choose to experience negative emotions over positive ones when understanding the difference and implications? One more question: What would cause you to consider and choose to experience negative emotions over positive emotions when you are in control of your thoughts, emotions, and behaviors? Just a Thought!!!

In the context of awareness and deliberation when speaking of forgiveness, it is distinct from excusing or reconciling with the one who caused the hurt. Did you hear that, forgiveness is not excusing? To release someone as part of forgiveness is to let go of the wish for revenge or retribution; it's a release of the power they hold over your emotional state. This release is critical because it signifies a shift in control — from being a victim of the hurt to becoming the architect of your healing. It means no longer allowing the offender's actions to dictate your feelings, decisions, or sense of peace. This also does not mean you condone what happened or that you must re-establish a relationship with the offender. It simply means that you are choosing to free yourself from the negative emotional ties that bind you to the past and the offender. I love the art of forgiveness, what a powerful process to restore you.

So, making a conscious decision to forgive involves a deep awareness of the hurt and the emotions it has stimulated, a courageous choice to move forward in the healing process, and a nuanced understanding of what forgiveness means for one's own peace and well-being. It is about acknowledging the difficulty of the journey while remaining committed to the path, understanding the personal implications of forgiveness, and choosing to release the offender from your emotional world. I will always reiterate that this process can be challenging but ultimately empowering, leading to a state of emotional freedom and a more peaceful, fulfilling life.

Can you see the power in saying such words as "I forgive you", "I forgive you for the words you spoke against and to me that caused me so much pain", I forgive you for the actions and decisions you made that caused me to question who I am", "I forgive you". The power is activated in your intentionality and purpose. Say the words, not just in your mind but allow yourself to hear the words that you are working towards.

Intentionality and Purpose are the cornerstones of making a conscious decision to forgive. This means that forgiveness is not a passive act that happens to someone; rather, it is an active choice, a deliberate commitment to a path that leads away from emotional harm but a move toward healing. When an individual decides to forgive, they do so with the understanding that while the journey is not without its challenges, the outcome — a life marked by less anger, improved mental health, and greater emotional freedom — is inherently valuable and desirable. The decision to forgive is thus a decision to prioritize and put you first intentionally. Forgiveness does not happen by happenstance.

The intentionality behind forgiveness involves a clear recognition of its benefits. Reduced anger and resentment lead to a calmer, more balanced life, allowing individuals to respond to new situations with clarity and composure rather than through the lens of past hurts-sometimes called psychological strongholds. Improved mental health is another significant benefit, as letting go of grudges and negative feelings can decrease stress, anxiety, and depression, leading to a more joyful and content existence. Lastly, emotional freedom is perhaps the most profound benefit of all. This does not just mean freedom from negative emotions related to past hurt, but also the freedom to experience and enjoy life fully, to engage in relationships without the heavy baggage of unresolved issues, and to open oneself up to new experiences and possibilities. Imagine intentionally choosing to forgive with the understanding of the benefits; that is not selfish, that's wisdom.

Choosing forgivenes is therefore a purposeful act of self-care and self-respect. It is about acknowledging that while the pain was real and its impact significant, continuing to carry the burden of unforgiveness serves no constructive purpose. I want to say that again, UNFORGIVENESS SERVES NO CONSTRUCTIVE PURPOSE. Instead, by intentionally choosing to forgive, individuals take a powerful step towards creating a life defined not by what has happened to them, but by their aspirations, values, and the pursuit of a more peaceful and fulfilling life. Here it is again, this *choice* is a testament to your strength, resilience, and enduring commitment and to your own health and happiness. Remember- You can have it, simply commit to the process, and refuse to quit.

Commitment to the Process: Choosing to forgive consciously also involves a commitment to the process. It means being prepared to engage with the emotions, to work through the layers of hurt, and to continually reaffirm the decision to forgive, especially when faced with setbacks or when the emotional pain resurfaces as some of the emotions have layers, it doesn't mean you haven't done the work. Layers of unforgiveness can and often does cause layers of pain and hurt and thus the importance of taking your time to heal.

Remaining committed to the process at this juncture of forgiveness is a testament to your strength and resilience- this is growth and maturity. It is a courageous, conscious decision to engage deeply with your emotions, to work diligently through the layers of hurt, and to continually reaffirm the commitment to heal and move forward, particularly when it appears there are setbacks or when the emotional pain resurfaces. This commitment does not just demonstrate endurance; it reflects a profound sense of empowerment and honor for who you are and the strength you possess. It is about recognizing that while the journey may be challenging, the ultimate reward of emotional freedom and peace is invaluable, and you possess what it takes to achieve the prize of freedom from the torment and all its emotions.

I think it is important to acknowledge that the journey of forgiveness is not a path walked once, but a road continuously traveled with intention and heart. It requires an open and compassionate engagement with your own emotions, being honest, an acceptance of the non-linear nature of healing, and a level of persistent dedication to the fulfillment of your goals to reach freedom. This process might involve revisiting painful memories or confronting lingering bitterness, yet with each step, you will grow stronger, more understanding, and more capable of love and empathy — both for yourself and for others. I can't say it enough that the conscious choice to forgive is a powerful act of freedom, freeing you from the bonds of past hurt and opening up a future rich with possibilities, hope, and opportunities.

I know you may be stuck on the fact that I said that the journey to forgiveness is not a path walked once but a road continuously traveled with intention and with heart. Whenever we are engaged in relationships with people the chance of getting hurt is possible. Learning to choose forgiveness will help with your mental and emotional maintenance. I don't want you to think that once we're healed it's impossible to happen again. I don't want you to isolate yourself or be weary of people. Generally speaking, people don't engage to cause harm.

Choosing to forgive is therefore a type of pursuit that involves cultivating supportive practices, seeking understanding, and sometimes professional guidance to navigate the complexities of emotional healing. It is an inspiring journey, marked not by the hurt that initiated it, but by an individual's unwavering commitment to their personal healing defined by their own terms of compassion, understanding, and profound emotional wisdom. This commitment to the forgiveness process is a beautiful, bold declaration of one's capacity for transformation and a life lived with intention and grace.

Let's look at what making a conscious decision looks like in action:

1. **Self-Reflection**: First and foremost, self-reflection is a powerful tool often underutilized. During self-reflection an individual might spend time journaling or meditating, contemplating and evaluating the impact of the hurt and the potential benefits of forgiveness. During self- reflection they weigh the cost of holding onto resentment against the promise of peace that forgiveness offers.

2. **Seeking Support**: Making the conscious decision to forgive might also involve seeking support from friends, family, or professionals. This can include discussing the decision, exploring

its implications, and gathering strength and encouragement from others. A support system is always valuable when navigating the multifaceted process of forgiveness.

3. **Establishing a Plan**: Sometimes, making a conscious decision to forgive involves establishing a plan or strategy for how to approach the process. This might include setting specific goals, such as writing a letter of forgiveness (not required to send), practicing empathy and understanding towards the offender, or engaging in activities that promote emotional release and healing such as exercising or volunteering. Ensure you have a journal during this process. A journal allows you to not only see your progress and celebrate but also allows you to see where you may need to adjust. Journaling also helps to take your thoughts from your mind, freeing up space for more thoughtful thinking and processing.

4. **Practicing Affirmations**: Some may choose to reinforce their decision through affirmations, making decrees and declarations that remind themselves of their commitment to forgive and the reasons behind it, along with decreeing and declaring positive thoughts daily about who they are and where they are headed on this journey. Others might engage in a ritual, such as a symbolic letting go of emotions of their decision to forgive, to mark the beginning of their journey. An example of this could be placing a chair in front of you and speaking as if the person were present and sharing your thoughts, feelings, and emotions. You could also write a letter but not send it, or you could have someone you trust to stand in as the person who hurt you and allow you to speak to them as if they were present. You get to make choices of how you work the process. Remember, whatever you practice you become, thus ensure you

include practicing forgiveness and the attributes coupled with it.

BOTTOM LINE: TRUST THE PROCESS

Trusting the process of forgiveness is an essential component of making a conscious decision to forgive. Remember the process is not straight just as a highway or interstate is not straight, it gets congested, you make decisions, but you always arrive. Trusting the forgiveness process may involve a few setbacks, difficult emotions, and a gradual release of hurt and resentment as opposed to it being sudden. Trusting the process means remaining committed to the path of forgiveness, even when it feels challenging or when progress seems slow. It is about having faith that the journey, though difficult, will lead to the desired outcome of greater peace and emotional freedom.

It is a declaration of one's commitment to the rewarding journey involving awareness, intentionality, and a trust in the process, guided by the belief that the path of forgiveness, though diverse with difficulty, offers the promise of emotional freedom.

CHAPTER 4

FORGIVENESS IN THE MIND AND HEART

F orgiving others, especially in the wake of deep hurt or betrayal, is often a challenging endeavor. Understanding why forgiveness is difficult can be crucial in helping individuals navigate their path to healing and emotional freedom. The complexity of forgiveness involves multiple facets of the human experience, including relational dynamics, emotional processes, and cognitive functioning.

RELATIONSHIPS AND THE HEART AND SOUL OF MAN

1. **Emotional Connection and Betrayal**: Relationships are often the bedrock of our emotional lives. When someone we trust betrays us, it does not just break a rule; it shatters a bond. The heart and soul, representing our deepest feelings and values, are profoundly affected. This emotional rupture creates a pain that goes beyond the surface, touching the core of our being, making forgiveness difficult.

2. **Identity and Self-Worth**: Relationships contribute significantly to our sense of identity and self-worth. When these relationships are damaged, it often leads to a profound sense of loss and questioning of one's self-worth. Forgiving can sometimes feel

like letting go of a part of one's identity, which sometimes is built around hurt and betrayal.

3. **The Quest for Justice**: At a soulful level, there's often a deep-seated need for justice or retribution. Forgiveness might be perceived as giving up on this quest, leading to a feeling of moral defeat or the fear of condoning the hurtful behavior.

THE MIND AND ITS RESPONSE TO HURT

1. **Cognitive Biases**: The human mind is wired to protect us from harm, and this includes psychological harm. When hurt occurs, it can cause cognitive distortions and ruminations which can intensify and prolong feelings of anger and resentment. These biases can cause individuals to focus on the negative aspects of the situation, making it harder to perceive the potential benefits of forgiveness. Their thought processes and decision-making often become shaped by the hurt.

2. **Memory and Emotional Encoding**: Emotional memories, especially those related to hurtful events, are strongly encoded in the brain. These memories can easily be triggered, bringing back the pain and anger as if the event just occurred. These strong emotional memories make it difficult to let go and forgive, as the mind continually relives the hurt.

3. **Fear of Vulnerability**: Forgiving can sometimes be perceived as opening oneself up to further hurt. The mind, in its attempt to protect, may resist forgiveness to avoid potential vulnerability. This resistance is often subconscious, making the process of forgiving even more challenging.

Forgiveness is an emotional and cognitive act that involves the heart, mind, and the will of a person. It's not enough to intellectually decide to forgive; for forgiveness to be complete and effective, it must be felt and integrated emotionally.

As we can see forgiveness is so much more complex than we thought. Forgiveness is indeed a multifaceted process involving both the cognitive and emotional realms of our being. Cognitively, forgiveness involves the mind, which is the seat of our thoughts, consciousness, decision-making, and perception. It is where we intellectually understand the need to forgive, recognize the benefits of letting go, and consciously deciding to embark on the forgiveness journey. Cognition involves all mental activities, including reasoning, memory, attention, and problem-solving. Thought patterns are the habitual ways we think, often developed over time, which can significantly impact our emotional well-being and our tendency towards or against forgiveness.

However, true forgiveness extends beyond singularly our cognitive understanding or mental decision making. It involves the heart, which symbolically represents the center of our emotions and feelings. Emotions are complex responses to internal or external events, significantly influencing our behavior, thought processes, and overall mental state. For forgiveness to be complete and transformative, it must be integrated emotionally — it requires genuinely feeling the release of resentment, the softening of anger and the cultivation of empathy and compassion towards the offender and oneself.

The emotional aspect of forgiveness is critical because unforgiveness is often rooted in and sustained by deep-seated negative emotions. As discussed earlier, these can include feelings of anger, resentment, bitterness, hatred, spite, and a desire for revenge. Unforgiveness can also lead to sadness, depression, or a sense of betrayal and loss. Each of these emotions, if left unaddressed, can create an internal environment of chronic stress and negativity, affecting not only mental and emotional health but physical well-being too. Yes, unforgiveness can and often does settle in the systems of the body, especially the digestive system. Therefore, while the decision to forgive might be initiated in the mind, it is in the heart where it finds its depth and healing power. Integrating forgiveness emotionally means allowing these feelings to transform, actively cultivating positive emotions like empathy, understanding, and ultimately, peace. Empathy will not be found in every situation; however, in some situations you will experience a level or degree of empathy dependent upon the person and the situation. It is a journey that engages the full spectrum of our human experience, leading to a more harmonious and liberated state of being.

Hurtful acts and words possess a profound power to activate deep emotional and cognitive responses, engaging both the heart and the mind in a state of unforgiveness. When we are wronged, our mind quickly processes the act or words as threats or injustices, leading to a series of cognitive responses including shock, denial, or a heightened state of alertness. These mental activities often go hand-in-hand with a narrative of hurt, betrayal, or injustice that keeps replaying, reinforcing the pain and the memory of the offense. Our thoughts become consumed by the event, continuously triggering, and amplifying the emotional responses.

Simultaneously, our heart, the center of our emotional world, reacts with a surge of feelings. Words, often carrying deep emotional significance, can wound as sharply as physical acts, invoking strong emotions such as anger, sadness, betrayal, and resentment. These emotions are not just brief responses; they can settle deep within us, becoming a persistent state that colors our entire emotional world. The hurt and pain, continually activated by memories and thoughts of the offense, create an emotional loop that fuels the state of unforgiveness. The intensity of these emotions is a manifestation exhibited by the power of hurtful words and acts that wound our psyche deeply. This cycle of cognitive and emotional activation not only sustains unforgiveness but can also lead to long-term psychological and physical distress if not addressed and resolved. Recognizing the impact of hurtful acts and words on both the mind and heart is crucial in understanding the persistence of unforgiveness and the importance of engaging in the healing process.

CHAPTER 5

ACTS OR BEHAVIORS THAT CAN CAUSE HARM

ehaviors that cause hurt and lead to unforgiveness are often those that violate personal, moral, or social expectations in a significant way. The resulting hurt can be profound, leaving lasting emotional scars and fostering a wide range of negative feelings. Here are some common behaviors that tend to cause such hurt and potentially lead to unforgiveness:

BETRAYAL

- **Infidelity**: In romantic relationships, infidelity is a common cause of deep hurt and often leads to unforgiveness. The breach of trust and the intimate nature of the betrayal can be particularly damaging.
- **External Relational Betrayal**: sometimes referred to as backstabbing- Betrayal in friendships, such as abandoning the relationship without understanding, sharing confidential information, talking behind one's back, or siding with an adversary. Each of these can destroy the foundation of trust and lead to longstanding resentment and unforgiveness. can destroy the foundation of trust and lead to long-standing resentment and unforgiveness.

Though betrayal shown through infidelity and backstabbing are the most common, betrayal can manifest in various forms beyond infidelity and backstabbing, deeply affecting personal trust and relationships. Here are a few other examples of betrayal:

- **Financial Betrayal**: This could involve stealing money, engaging in fraudulent activities at someone else's expense, or abusing someone's trust for financial gain, especially when you know the person. It might also include breaking promises related to financial agreements or commitments.
- **Emotional Betrayal**: This type of betrayal occurs when someone reveals or uses sensitive information shared in confidence against the person. It can also include manipulating someone's feelings for personal gain or advantage.
- **Professional Betrayal**: This happens in the workplace or business relationships and can include taking credit for someone else's work, sabotaging a colleague's efforts, or breaking confidentiality about professional dealings.
- **Social Betrayal**: This involves damaging someone's social standing or relationships through gossip, slander, or spreading false information. It can also include publicly humiliating someone or revealing private information without consent.
- **Betrayal of Trust**: At its core, any action or inaction that significantly undermines the trust another person has placed in an individual can be seen as a betrayal. This might include failing to support a friend or family member during a critical time or not keeping significant promises.

These examples underscore that betrayal can occur in various contexts and relationships, each with its nuances and implications. Regardless of the form it takes, betrayal is a profound breach of trust and can lead to significant emotional and psychological distress. This is not an exhaustive list but examples to help with understanding through means that unforgiveness takes root.

DECEPTION AND LIES

Deception and lies are potent forms of betrayal that can deeply erode trust and lead to unforgiveness. When an individual engages in deceit, they are intentionally misleading or concealing the truth. They create a false narrative that can have serious emotional, relational, or even financial repercussions for the deceived. Lies, whether small or substantial, chip away at the foundation of trust that relationships are built upon, leaving feelings of betrayal, anger, and hurt in the wake of their aftermath. The discovery of such dishonesty often shocks and disorients the person deceived, leading to a questioning of reality and a reevaluation of the relationship. The pain and disillusionment caused by deception are profound, as they not only damage the present relationship but can also instill a lasting wariness and skepticism in the deceived person, affecting their future interactions and ability to trust others. Consequently, the deep-seated hurt and breach of trust caused by deception and lies make them significant behaviors leading to unforgiveness, as the injured person struggles to reconcile the pain with the act of letting go.

- **Dishonesty**: Being lied to or deceived, especially repeatedly, can lead to feelings of mistrust and hurt. It can make the deceived person question their judgment and the sincerity of their relationship with the deceiver. Once discovered, it often leads to unforgiveness.
- **Fraud and Scams**: Being the victim of fraud, scams, or any form of financial deceit not only causes financial harm but also emotional distress, leading to unforgiveness.

ABUSE

Abuse, in its many forms — whether physical, emotional, psychological, or sexual — is a severe and destructive behavior that often leads to deep-seated unforgiveness. It represents a profound violation of the victim's body, mind, and spirit, undermining their sense of safety, self-worth, and trust in others. The insidious nature of abuse lies in its repetitive and controlling aspects, often trapping the victim in a cycle of fear, shame, and degradation. The traumatic impact of such experiences doesn't just linger; it can fundamentally alter one's outlook on relationships and life, leading to long-term emotional and psychological scars. Victims of abuse frequently grapple with intense feelings of anger, betrayal, and resentment, which are justified responses to having their dignity and autonomy violated. These powerful emotions, coupled with the possible physical reminders of the abuse, make forgiveness extraordinarily challenging. The path to forgiving an abuser is complex and deeply personal, requiring significant emotional work and often professional support to navigate the layers of hurt and trauma. Therefore, abuse stands as a stark and harrowing behavior that can significantly hinder the capacity and willingness to forgive, reflecting the need for a careful, compassionate approach to healing and recovery.

- **Physical Abuse**: Physical violence or abuse is a direct assault on one's person and safety, leading to deep physical and emotional wounds, often accompanied by a lasting sense of fear and resentment which produces unforgiveness.
- **Emotional or Psychological Abuse**: This can include manipulation, controlling behavior, constant criticism, or any other form of psychological harm. Due to its covert nature, it can be particularly dangerous and damaging.

- **Neglect**: Especially in dependent relationships like parent-child or caregiver-dependent, neglect can lead to significant emotional pain and feelings of worthlessness. Such childhood trauma often manifests more emotionally in relationships during adulthood.

DISCRIMINATION AND PREJUDICE

Discrimination and prejudice are deeply ingrained behaviors that can lead to pervasive and lasting unforgiveness due to their targeted, often systemic nature of marginalizing and oppressing individuals based on their race, ethnicity, gender, sexuality, religion, or other inherent characteristics. These behaviors not only inflict immediate hurt and exclusion but also perpetuate a broader culture of inequality and injustice, contributing to the continuous emotional and psychological harm of affected communities. The pain inflicted by discrimination and prejudice is not just personal; it is a shared burden that resonates with collective experiences of historical and ongoing injustice. This complex layering of personal and communal hurt, coupled with the often unacknowledged or unaddressed nature of such biases, makes forgiveness exceedingly difficult. Victims of discrimination and prejudice must navigate not only the personal journey of healing from direct offenses but also the larger, ongoing struggle against the societal structures that enable such behaviors. The path to forgiving acts of discrimination and prejudice is, therefore, intertwined with the broader pursuit of recognition, justice, and systemic change, making it a uniquely challenging and emotionally charged aspect of the forgiveness process.

Racism, Sexism, or Any Form of Discrimination can have major mental health implications. Being the target of discrimination or prejudice attacks the very core of one's identity, leading to profound hurt and often a lasting sense of injustice and anger. Many find it difficult to get forgiveness when there is racism, sexism, or discrimination due to the social/emotional stigma attached.

REJECTION

Rejection, whether in personal relationships, professional settings, or broader social contexts, is a profound experience that often leads to unforgiveness due to its direct impact on one's sense of self-worth and belonging. The act of being dismissed, excluded, or deemed unworthy can invoke deep feelings of hurt, sadness, and inadequacy, leaving emotional scars that are difficult to heal. The pain of rejection is particularly heartbreaking because it directly touches on our fundamental human need for connection and acceptance. Whether it is a romantic breakup, a friend turning away, a job refusal, or social exclusion, the message that one is not wanted or valued can have a lasting effect, leading to pervasive feelings of bitterness and resentment. These feelings are often compounded by the circumstances surrounding the rejection, such as a lack of closure or understanding, which can leave individuals ruminating over the incident and struggling to move past the hurt. As a result, rejection is also a potent behavior leading to unforgiveness, as individuals grapple with the emotional fallout and the challenge of rebuilding their self-esteem and trust in others. The journey to overcoming the hurt of rejection and finding a path to forgiveness is deeply personal, often requiring time, self-compassion, and sometimes the support of others to navigate the complex emotions involved.

- **Personal Rejection**: Being rejected by a loved one, a friend, or even a community can lead to feelings of abandonment and hurt. This is especially potent if the rejection is handled insensitively or suddenly. Roots of rejection will always produce unforgiveness.

- **Professional Rejection**: Workplace mistreatment, unfair dismissal, undermining, disrespect, or constant criticism can lead to feelings of inadequacy and resentment. Leadership and management training often leave out the role unforgiveness plays in workplace relationships, team building, productivity, and psychological safety. It's critical that we begin to address this phenomenon in the workplace as it is the culprit of most relational workplace challenges.

PUBLIC HUMILIATION

Public humiliation is a particularly devastating behavior that can lead to deep-seated unforgiveness, primarily due to its invasive and exposing nature. When someone is humiliated in public, their dignity is stripped away in front of others, magnifying the hurt and embarrassment. This type of behavior does not just inflict emotional pain in the moment; it leaves a lasting mark on the individual's self-esteem and reputation, often replaying in the person's mind and reinforcing feelings of shame and inadequacy. The public aspect of the humiliation means that the incident is not just a personal memory but potentially a shared one, complicating the individual's social interactions and sense of safety in communal spaces. The violation of privacy and the forced vulnerability can lead to deep anger, resentment, and mistrust towards the perpetrator, as well as a pervasive sense of injustice and desire for vindication. Overcoming the intense emotions associated with public humiliation and moving towards forgiveness is a significant challenge, requiring not just a personal reconciliation with the event but often a reclamation of one's public image and sense of self in the aftermath of such a deeply public and personal offense.

Being publicly ridiculed or shamed, whether in a personal, professional, or online setting, can lead to deep embarrassment and hurt, often harboring long-term resentment and anger that is produced from the unforgiveness.

AGGRESSION AND HOSTILITY

Aggression and hostility are behaviors that significantly contribute to unforgiveness due to their direct, often forceful violation of personal respect and safety. Aggressive behaviors, whether verbal assaults, threatening postures, or physical violence, invoke an immediate defensive response and leave a lasting impression of fear, anger, and hurt. Hostility, whether expressed through sarcasm, contempt, or outright rage, communicates a lack of regard for the well-being and dignity of the other person. These behaviors not only cause immediate harm but also corrode the foundation of trust and respect necessary for healthy relationships. The targeted individual is left to grapple with feelings of vulnerability, injustice, and resentment, often revisiting the incidents and the emotions they provoke. Aggression and hostility can sever bonds, create emotional barriers, and leave deep psychological scars that make the prospect of forgiveness daunting. Overcoming the impact of such behaviors requires significant emotional resilience and often a desire to protect oneself from future harm, making the journey toward forgiving of these acts a challenging and deeply personal endeavor.

- **Verbal Attacks**: Insults, aggressive language, or threats can create an environment of fear and hostility, leading to emotional distress and resentment.
- **Bullying**: Persistent bullying, whether in childhood or as an adult, can lead to significant psychological trauma and feelings of anger and unforgiveness.

For those who have been hurt by such behaviors, the journey towards healing and potentially forgiving these transgressions involve recognizing and validating their pain, understanding the impact of the hurtful behavior, and finding ways to process and release the associated negative emotions. For those who have caused the hurt, genuinely acknowledging the harm done, expressing remorse, and making amends are crucial in mending the damage and moving toward reconciliation. In all cases, the process is deeply personal and can be significantly aided by empathetic support and, in some or most cases, professional counseling.

CHAPTER 6

THE HARM CAUSED BY WORDS

The harm caused by words is profound and can often lead to deep-seated hurt and unforgiveness. Unlike physical wounds, which tend to heal over time, the wounds caused by hurtful words can linger in the mind and heart, sometimes indefinitely. This type of harm is particularly dangerous because it can affect individuals' perceptions of themselves, their relationships, and their view of the world around them. Here's a closer look at the harm caused by words and their connection to hurt and unforgiveness:

PSYCHOLOGICAL AND EMOTIONAL IMPACT

The psychological and emotional impact of negative words can and often lead to a state of unforgiveness, particularly due to the deep and lasting impression that such words can imprint on an individual's psyche. Derogatory, demeaning, or critical language can significantly damage self-esteem, instill feelings of worthlessness, and provoke long-term emotional distress. Words, especially when used to manipulate, belittle, or degrade, carry immense power to shape one's self-perception and worldview.

The pain inflicted by hurtful language is not easily forgotten; it lingers in the form of memories and reinforced negative thought patterns, continually affecting mood, behavior, and well-being. The recipient of such words might find themselves trapped in a cycle of rumination and resentment, struggling to release the grip of past insults or criticisms. The betrayal felt when someone uses words as weapons, particularly if that person is a trusted friend, family member, or authority figure, can profoundly erode trust and complicate the path to forgiveness. Consequently, the psychological and emotional impact of negative words is a pervasive force that can lead to an enduring state of unforgiveness, necessitating a conscientious effort to heal and reclaim one's sense of self.

- **Self-Esteem and Self-Worth**: Hurtful words can significantly impact an individual's self-esteem and sense of self-worth. Insults, criticisms, or demeaning language can lead individuals to internalize negative messages about themselves, affecting their confidence and how they interact with the world.
- **Mental Health**: Repeated exposure to hurtful language can lead to anxiety, depression, and other mental health issues. It can create a persistent state of emotional turmoil and stress, affecting overall well-being.
- **Trauma and Stress**: Particularly abusive or threatening language can be traumatic, leading to conditions such as post-traumatic stress disorder (PTSD). The individual might relive the words and experience intense stress and anxiety long after the incident.

INTERPERSONAL RELATIONSHIPS

Interpersonal relationships can be severely damaged by negative words, leading to a lasting state of unforgiveness. When hurtful, critical, or demeaning language is used between individuals, it can fracture the trust and respect that form the foundation of the relationship. Negative words can inflict deep emotional wounds, creating barriers of resentment and mistrust that are difficult to overcome. The intimacy and closeness once shared can be replaced with distance and caution, as the aggrieved person guards against further emotional harm. The impact of such words is often compounded in close relationships, where the expectation for support and understanding is betrayed. This betrayal can lead to a persistent questioning of the other person's regards and intentions, making every interaction colored by past hurts. The reluctance to forgive in these instances is rooted in the fear of being vulnerable again and the challenge of rebuilding what was once broken. As a result, negative words within interpersonal relationships can create a lasting rift, with unforgiveness serving as a protective but isolating barrier against further emotional injury.

- **Trust and Safety**: Hurtful words can break down trust and feelings of safety in a relationship. When someone is repeatedly hurt by words, they may find it difficult to trust others or feel safe in future interactions, leading to isolation or strained relationships.
- **Communication Breakdown**: When hurtful language is used, it can lead to a breakdown in communication. The injured party may withdraw or retaliate with hurtful words of their own, leading to escalating conflicts and a cycle of hurt.
- **Reputation and Social Standing**: Slanderous or gossiping language can damage an individual's reputation and standing within a community, leading to social isolation and emotional distress.

LONGEVITY OF EMOTIONAL WOUNDS

The longevity of personal wounds inflicted by negative words contributes significantly to a state of unforgiveness, particularly as the pain and memories linger and continue to affect an individual's emotional well-being long after the words are spoken. Hurtful, critical, or demeaning remarks can embed themselves in the psyche, becoming a part of one's inner dialogue and self-perception. The durability of these wounds is often due to the intimate and personal nature of words; they can be tailored to target an individual's most vulnerable attributes, making the hurt particularly poignant and difficult to dismiss.

Over time, these wounds can fester, leading to a chronic state of resentment, low self-esteem, and bitterness. The individual may relive the moments of hurt repeatedly, each time re-experiencing the emotional pain and reinforcing the difficulty of forgiving the perpetrator. The enduring nature of such wounds demands a significant effort to heal, involving not only a reassessment of the hurtful words and their impact but also a conscious effort to reconstruct a more positive and resilient sense of self. Consequently, the longevity and personal nature of wounds caused by negative words make them powerful and persistent source of unforgiveness, requiring time, introspection, and often external support to overcome.

- **Long-lasting Impact**: Unlike physical wounds that heal and fade, the emotional wounds caused by hurtful words can last a lifetime. Individuals might replay the words in their minds, each time re-experiencing the hurt and reinforcing negative feelings and beliefs about themselves or others. These types of emotional wounds can cause a person to never become who they desired or live the life they always wanted. Forgiveness is critical when words cause the pain.
- **Difficulty in Healing**: Emotional wounds from words are often invisible to others, making them difficult to address and heal. The individual might feel that their pain is not taken seriously

or that they should just "get over it," further complicating the healing process.

UNFORGIVENESS AND BITTERNESS

Unforgiveness and bitterness often stem from negative words that cut deep into the fabric of one's emotional well-being, creating a long-lasting state of resentment and anger. When someone is subjected to derogatory, critical, or dismissive language, it can provoke a profound sense of injustice and hurt, leading to an inability or unwillingness to forgive. The words linger, echoing in the mind, reinforcing feelings of bitterness and unforgiveness which become hard to uproot. This emotional state can become a pervasive aspect of one's life, shading interactions with others and one's overall outlook. More critical, it can keep them stuck for a lifetime. Bitterness can become a part of their very character.

The bitterness felt is not just a reaction to the words themselves but a continuous response to the ongoing emotional pain they cause. It can hinder personal growth, affect relationships, and lead to a cyclical pattern of negativity and mistrust. The challenge then becomes not just about overcoming the initial hurt, or the initial unforgiveness but also addressing the deep-rooted bitterness that prevents moving forward. Breaking this cycle requires recognizing the impact of these words, consciously choosing to release the associated negative emotions, and engaging in emotional healing to overcome the pervasive state of unforgiveness.

- **Resistance to Forgiveness**: The deep hurt caused by words can lead to unforgiveness, where the injured party holds onto resentment and anger. This unforgiveness can be a protective mechanism, guarding against further hurt, but it can also lead to bitterness and prolonged suffering.

- **Cycle of Hurt**: Unforgiveness can create a cycle of hurt, where the injured party might harbor resentment and anger for years, affecting their well-being and relationships. It can also lead to retaliatory behavior, perpetuating a cycle of hurt and unforgiveness. You can become what you hate.

Because of the significant harm caused by words, it is crucial to be mindful of the language we use and its potential impact on others. Encouraging open and compassionate communication, seeking to understand and empathize with the hurt caused, and working towards genuine apologies and forgiveness are all important steps in addressing the harm caused by words and moving toward healing and reconciliation. Additionally, individuals who have been hurt by words might benefit from seeking support from friends, family, or professionals as stated earlier, who can help them navigate their feelings and work towards healing.

CHAPTER 7

SCARS OF UNFORGIVENESS

T he scars associated with unforgiveness, and conversely, those that result or heal through forgiveness, are deeply etched emotional, and sometimes physical reminders of past hurt and pain. They represent the lasting impact of significant emotional experiences and can significantly influence an individual's well-being, relationships, and overall life trajectory. Understanding these scars is crucial to comprehending the full scope of forgiveness and unforgiveness.

The scars of unforgiveness, especially those stemming from negative words, penetrate deep into the realm of emotional, physical, and spiritual well-being, manifesting in various debilitating forms. These scars are not merely reminders of past hurts but are active components in shaping one's current and future state of being.

Emotional Turmoil: The most immediate and apparent scars of unforgiveness are those of emotional turmoil. Negative words can instill lasting feelings of anger, resentment, and bitterness. These emotions, when held onto, create an inner environment of constant turmoil, where peace and joy are overshadowed by the persistent shadow of past hurts. This emotional unrest is not static; it fluctuates and often intensifies with reminders or additional perceived slights, making personal happiness and emotional stability elusive targets.

Unforgiveness keeps the emotional wounds open, leading to ongoing pain, anger, resentment, and bitterness. These emotions can become a chronic state of being, affecting mood, outlook on life, and interactions with others.

Physical Health: The impact of unforgiveness extends beyond the emotional and mental into the physical realm. The chronic stress associated with harboring resentment and bitterness can lead to a myriad of health issues, including hypertension, heart disease, weakened immune function, and exacerbated symptoms of existing conditions. The body's stress response, designed to handle immediate threats can operate as if you are always in crisis. The stress and negativity of unforgiveness can manifest physically. It is linked to increased anxiety, depression, and stress, which in turn can affect cardiovascular health, immune function, and overall well-being. The body's continual state of alertness and tension can lead to long-term health issues and is not equipped for the continuous activation caused by unforgiveness, leading to wear and tear that manifests physically. Hence, the reluctance to forgive, while seemingly an emotional stance, has tangible, detrimental effects on physical health. The stress and negativity of unforgiveness will always manifest physically; despite your awareness. Again, the body's continual state of alertness and tension can lead to long-term health issues.

Impaired Relationships: Unforgiveness, particularly in response to negative words, can severely damage relationships. The trust and openness required for healthy relationships are undermined by the suspicion and hostility that unforgiveness breeds. This can lead to a breakdown in communication, emotional distancing, and even the end of relationships. Moreover, bitterness and mistrust can spill over into other relationships, affecting one's overall ability to connect with and trust others. The individual may become more guarded and less likely to engage in new relationships, leading to a cycle of isolation and loneliness. Unforgiveness commonly leads to strained or broken relationships, it is a rarity for it not to have adverse implications. It often creates walls between individuals, preventing reconciliation, understanding, and intimacy. The mistrust and hurt often bleed into other relationships, affecting one's overall social life and connection with others both personally and professionally.

Stunted Personal Growth: Holding onto unforgiveness acts as a barrier to personal development. The mental and emotional energy consumed by resentment and bitterness diverts focus and resources away from growth and self-improvement. Opportunities for learning from past experiences, developing empathy, and gaining deeper self-awareness are lost amidst the preoccupation with past hurts. The individual's worldview may become increasingly negative and limited, stifling creativity, optimism, and the pursuit of personal goals and happiness. Holding onto unforgiveness can keep individuals stuck in the past, preventing them from moving forward and experiencing personal growth. The energy and attention given to the hurt and the person who caused it can stifle development and limit opportunities for new experiences and relationships.

Spiritual and Mental Well-Being: Finally, unforgiveness can profoundly impact one's spiritual and mental well-being. Spiritually, it can create a sense of disconnection or conflict, especially for those whose beliefs emphasize the importance of forgiveness and compassion. The spiritual dissonance between one's values and actions can lead to feelings of guilt, shame, and spiritual unrest. Mentally, the continuous focus on negative emotions and past events can contribute to a range of psychological issues, including depression, anxiety, and a pervasive sense of dissatisfaction with life as previously stated. The inability to let go and move forward keeps the individual in a state of mental and spiritual stagnation, where healing and peace are continually out of reach. Unforgiveness can lead to spiritual distress, especially for those for whom forgiveness is a significant spiritual or moral value. Mentally, the ongoing rumination and negative emotions can contribute to psychological disorders or exacerbate existing conditions.

The scars of unforgiveness are multifaceted and deeply entrenched, affecting every aspect of an individual's life. They create a complex web of emotional, physical, relational, and spiritual challenges that can significantly diminish the quality of life. Recognizing and addressing these scars is crucial for anyone on the path to healing and seeking a more fulfilling and peaceful existence. Moving beyond the negative words and towards a state of forgiveness is not just an emotional release but a comprehensive act of self-healing and rejuvenation.

HEALING THE SCARS THROUGH FORGIVENESS

The healing of scars through forgiveness is a transformative journey that reverberates through all aspects of an individual's life, turning wounds into wisdom and pain into peace. When one embarks on the path of forgiveness, especially in response to the deep hurts caused by negative words, the healing manifests in various significant ways.

Emotional Release and Peace: Forgiveness facilitates a profound emotional release. Letting go of grudges, resentment, and bitterness liberates the individual from the heavy burden of negative emotions. This release is often accompanied by a newfound sense of peace and tranquility. The energy once consumed by maintaining feelings of unforgiveness is now available for positive, life-affirming emotions. People find themselves more capable of joy, love, and excitement for life. The emotional turmoil that once defined their daily existence gives way to a more serene and balanced emotional landscape. Choosing forgiveness is such a powerful emotional release of pent-up anger, resentment, and bitterness. You will find, as you navigate through the process, the reemerging of peace, relief, rest, and a state of contentment. During the emotional release, you begin to feel lighter as the burdens roll away and the chains are broken. Who wouldn't want this type of liberation? Is holding on to the pain worth the cost? Remember, forgiveness is about choosing, and this is a great place to pause if you haven't decided to release everyone who hurt you. It's not easy but it's worth it.

Improved Physical Health: The act of forgiving can lead to noticeable improvements in physical health. As the stress and negativity of unforgiveness dissipate, the body's stress response can normalize, reducing the risk of stress-related illnesses. Blood pressure can drop, sleep may improve, and overall energy levels can rise. The immune system, no longer suppressed by chronic stress, can function more effectively. In essence, forgiveness can halt the wear and tear on the body caused by prolonged emotional distress, leading to a healthier, more vibrant physical state. Forgiveness is associated with better physical health, including reduced stress and lower risk of chronic diseases. The act of forgiving can and does lead to decreased anxiety, improved sleep, and overall, a more positive health outlook. Unforgiveness is an anchor for emotional and psychological pain along with physical health issues.

Restored and Enhanced Relationships: Forgiveness often leads to the healing and sometimes restoration of relationships damaged by hurtful words and actions. By choosing to forgive, individuals open the door to understanding, empathy, and reconciliation. Even if the relationship does not return to its former state, forgiveness can transform the nature of the interaction from one of hostility and avoidance to one of civility and respect. Additionally, the act of forgiving sets a positive precedence for future relationships, enabling more open, honest, and compassionate connections. Forgiveness can lead to the restoration of relationships and the building of deeper, more understanding connections especially when it relates to family and friends. It opens the door to reconciliation and trust, allowing individuals to move forward together or apart, but with a sense of closure and peace.

Personal Empowerment and Growth: Choosing to forgive is an empowering act. It requires strength, maturity, and a deep sense of self-awareness. This process often leads to significant personal growth and maturity. Individuals who forgive learn a great deal about themselves, including their values, boundaries, and desires. They develop better coping strategies, become more resilient in the face of adversity, and often find a greater sense of purpose and direction in life. Forgiveness can be a catalyst for transformation, inspiring changes that lead to a more fulfilling and meaningful existence. Though it requires strength, empathy, and a broad perspective, you'll appreciate the positive outcome and impact on your character development. This process can enhance self-esteem, foster resilience, and open individuals to new understandings and possibilities. Are you ready for personal growth and development?

Spiritual Fulfillment and Mental Wellness: Finally, forgiveness can lead to profound spiritual fulfillment and mental wellness. Spiritually, it aligns individuals with values of compassion, understanding, and love. It provides a sense of peace and connection, both with oneself and a higher purpose or power. Mentally, the clarity and calmness that come with forgiveness can alleviate negative feelings and thoughts about self, leading to a more optimistic outlook. The mental space once occupied by negative thoughts and feelings is now free for creativity, problem-solving, and other constructive activities. Forgiveness can bring spiritual fulfillment, aligning individuals with their values and beliefs about compassion, love, and understanding not just towards others but yourself as we often struggle with forgiving ourselves more than others. Imagine mentally no longer being plagued by the pain and suffering that happened to you. Imagine waking up daily without the heavy burdens of negative thoughts and emotions. What might this feel like to wake up free, with a clear mind ready to create daily?

The healing of scars through forgiveness is a deeply restorative process. It touches every aspect of the individual's being, from their emotional state to their physical health, relationships, personal growth, and spiritual and mental wellness. While the journey to forgiveness can be challenging, especially in the face of deep-seated hurt from negative words, the rewards are immeasurable.

Remember, forgiveness is not just an act of letting go; it's a commitment to a healthier, happier, and more harmonious life. While forgiveness can significantly heal and transform, it's important to note that the scars may not disappear completely. They might remain as reminders of the past, but their impact on one's emotional and physical health can lessen significantly. The key is that these scars, instead of being sources of ongoing pain and resentment, become markers of resilience, growth, and the capacity to overcome and find peace. Whether one chooses to forgive or continues to struggle with unforgiveness, understanding the profound impact of these emotional scars is crucial in the journey toward healing and well-being. Emotional scars are often held in place by fear, therefore, it is another emotional hurdle that must be dealt with. Fear must be conquered. If it goes unconquered, it can hinder the restorative process of healing. Therefore, it is critical to acknowledge the attributes associated with fear that could hinder the restorative process.

CHAPTER 8

FEAR OF FORGIVING

T he fear of forgiving is a significant emotional hurdle that can hinder individuals from moving forward and healing from past hurts. This fear is often rooted in misconceptions about what forgiveness entails, concerns about the implications of forgiving, and the vulnerability associated with letting go of hurt. Here are several aspects of the fear of forgiveness:

1. Fear of Vulnerability

- **Opening Up to Further Hurt**: One of the primary fears is that by forgiving, one might open themselves up to further hurt. The act of forgiveness can sometimes be misconstrued as a sign of weakness or as an invitation for the offender to cause harm again.

- **Reliving the Pain**: Forgiving often involves revisiting the pain and hurt caused by the offense, not reliving the pain. Individuals might fear that in the process of forgiving, they will have to relive the trauma and emotional pain, which can be a daunting prospect. Revisiting the pain is not reliving the pain, as this time you get to look at what transpired as opposed to being in the moment and experiencing it. Revisiting the pain can be empowering in that you gain an understanding that the moment of the pain is just that, in the past. When you revisit the moment in time, you get to change the story. You get to revisit to change your current response. You no longer have to live with your initial response or you can choose a new response determined by what you now know.. You get to choose.

2. Fear of Injustice

- **Perceived Inequity**: As it relates to injustice, there is often a fear that forgiving someone means letting them "off the hook" or that the perpetrator will not face any consequences for their actions. This can feel like a grave injustice, particularly when the hurt caused is significant or life-altering. Forgiveness has never meant that the offender is not accountable, nor does it mean they should not take responsibility for their actions. Forgiveness is about breaking free from the pain of the incident so that you can live a life of freedom.
- **Undermining the Severity of the Hurt**: Some might fear that forgiving will somehow minimize or undermine the severity of the hurt they experienced. They worry that others might perceive their forgiveness as an indication that the offense was not that harmful or damaging.

3. Fear of Betraying Oneself or Values

- **Self-Betrayal**: For some, the idea of forgiving someone who has caused deep hurt feels like betraying themselves or their feelings. They may feel that they are being disloyal to themselves by even considering forgiveness.
- **Conflicting Values**: Sometimes, individuals might struggle with internal conflicts between their values (such as the importance of justice or standing up against wrong) and the concept of

forgiveness. This conflict can create a fear of compromising one's principles. To forgive is freedom, it does not compromise the integrity of who you are.

4. Fear of Changing Dynamics

- **Altering Relationships**: There is often a fear that forgiveness might lead to a shift in power dynamics, emotional distance, or the level of trust between the forgiving person and the one who offended. The greatest worry in this situation is becoming more vulnerable or the offender misrepresenting the forgiveness and using it to their advantage.
- **Loss of Control**: Holding onto unforgiveness can sometimes give individuals a sense of control over the situation or their emotions. The prospect of forgiving might feel like giving up this control, leading to uncertainty and fear.

ADVICE FOR OVERCOMING THE FEAR OF FORGIVING

1. **Understand Forgiveness**: Educating oneself about what forgiveness truly means and processing through one's fears is an important step as fear will hold unforgiveness in place. Remember, it is not about condoning the offense, forgetting it, or exposing oneself to further harm. Overcoming the fear of forgiveness is an act of profound courage, a pivotal step towards personal freedom and emotional healing. It acknowledges the strength to confront and transform the pain that held one hostage. Overcoming the fear associated with forgiving is a brave journey of releasing oneself and working towards truly reclaiming your power.

2. **Take It Slow**: Forgiveness does not have to be a one-time, all-or-nothing event. It can be a gradual process where one slowly works through the emotions and implications.

3. **Empowerment in Forgiveness**: Reframe forgiveness as an act of strength and self-care. It is a decision that can lead to personal empowerment and emotional freedom.

4. **Seek Support**: Don't hesitate to seek support from trusted friends, family members, or a professional therapist. Sometimes, having an external perspective can provide clarity and encouragement and advance the process. It's powerful when you can safely share your story without judgment or ridicule.

5. **Reflect on Benefits**: Consider the benefits of forgiveness, including reduced stress, improved mental health, and the possibility of restored or healthier relationships.

6. **Personal Growth**: Recognize that forgiving can be an opportunity for personal development and learning. It can lead to a deeper understanding of oneself and others.

By addressing the fears associated with forgiveness and taking steps to understand and confront these fears, individuals can begin to unlock the path to healing and moving forward. It is a deeply personal journey, and one that takes courage and compassion, but it is also a journey that can lead to significant emotional and psychological rewards.

CHAPTER 9

SELF FORGIVENESS

Moving from forgiving others to forgiving oneself is a crucial yet sometimes more challenging part of the healing journey. Often, individuals may find it easier to extend compassion and understanding to others while holding themselves to a higher, sometimes unforgiving standard. Self-forgiveness requires confronting one's own mistakes, failures, or perceived shortcomings with honesty and empathy. What Self-forgiveness is NOT; Self- forgiveness is not about you taking blame or responsibility for what someone else has done to you. It is about the mistakes that you have made consciously or unconsciously beating yourself up and refusing to forgive yourself for whatever reasons you have chosen. Self-forgiveness involves and begins with a deliberate choice to acknowledge these aspects without dwelling in a place of self-condemnation.

This process is often filled with internal resistance, as feelings of guilt, shame, and self-blame are deeply ingrained and protective, serving to align our actions with personal and societal values. However, when these feelings become persistent and self-punitive, they hinder growth, well-being, and happiness, making self-forgiveness a necessary path to reclaiming peace and self-compassion.

The difficulty in self-forgiveness often lies in the internal narrative that one constructs around their mistakes and identity. Overcoming this requires a shift in perspective, seeing errors as opportunities for learning and growth rather than as indelible stains on one's character. This perspective shift is a choice – a conscious decision to treat oneself with the same empathy and understanding one might offer a close friend. It involves recognizing that everyone is fallible, that mistakes are part of the human experience, and that one's worth is not defined by their worst moments. Engaging in self-forgiveness also means taking responsibility for one's actions, making amends where possible, and committing to better choices in the future. This active engagement with the process of self-forgiveness not only alleviates the burden of past regrets but also paves the way for a more authentic, compassionate, and fulfilling life. As difficult as it may be, choosing to forgive oneself is a profound act of self-love and a critical step toward lasting emotional and psychological health.

Self-forgiveness is an integral yet often overlooked aspect of the healing process. It is important to forgive oneself because self-forgiveness is crucial for emotional healing, personal growth, and overall well-being. It allows individuals to move past guilt and shame, learn from their mistakes, and embrace a more compassionate and positive self-view, fostering a healthier, more optimistic life outlook. You deserve to be forgiven just as everyone you have forgiven. Remember, it is a choice and a process, but you deserve it. Let us look at some of the challenges to self-forgiveness so that we can take away the excuses and change your belief system.

THE DIFFICULTY OF SELF-FORGIVENESS

Forgiving oneself can be more challenging than forgiving others. While you might offer grace and understanding to others, turning that compassion inward is often more complicated. Many individuals hold themselves to high standards and, when they fall short, plunge into self-criticism and harsh judgment. The intimate knowledge of one's thoughts and motivations can lead to a relentless replaying of mistakes, making self-forgiveness a difficult endeavor. This self-critique is often compounded by the belief that by not forgiving oneself, they are somehow making amends or punishing oneself, which one subconsciously feels is deserved.

SELF-BLAME AND ITS ROOTS

Self-blame is a common reaction to personal mistakes or failures. It is an attribution style where individuals attribute negative events to their deficiencies, or actions. In the context of trauma or hurt, victims might irrationally blame themselves for what happened, even when they were not responsible. This self-blame can be rooted in a desire for control, as it's often easier to believe that you had a role in causing the event (thereby suggesting you could have prevented it) than to accept the randomness or the actions of others, which leaves one feeling vulnerable and powerless.

GUILT AND SHAME

Guilt and shame are powerful emotions closely tied to self-forgiveness. Guilt arises from actions or behaviors that one perceives as wrong, leading to feelings of remorse and the desire to make amends. Shame, however, cuts deeper, affecting one's sense of self and worth. It is not just feeling bad about what you did; it is feeling bad about who you are. These feelings can be paralyzing, enveloping individuals in a cloud of unworthiness that makes self-forgiveness seem undeserved or unattainable.

EMBARRASSMENT AND ITS IMPLICATIONS

Embarrassment is another emotion linked to mistakes and social faux pas. While not as deep-seated as shame or guilt, embarrassment can still significantly impact one's willingness to forgive themselves. It involves a painful awareness of one's actions in the social context, leading to feelings of exposure and vulnerability. Overcoming embarrassment requires a reevaluation of the incident, understanding that everyone makes mistakes, and that these do not define one's entire character or worth.

HEALING THROUGH SELF-FORGIVENESS

1. **Acknowledge and Accept the Mistake**: The first step in self-forgiveness is acknowledging the mistake or wrongdoing without excusing it. This involves understanding what happened, why it happened, and accepting that it was a lapse in judgment or a result of specific circumstances.

2. **Understand the Emotions**: Dive deep into the emotions of guilt, shame, or embarrassment. Understand their origins and what they signify. At times, these emotions are exaggerated responses to the event, fueled by irrational beliefs about oneself.

3. **Challenge Negative Self-Talk**: Replace self-criticism with a more compassionate and realistic assessment of the situation. Remind yourself that everyone makes mistakes and that these do not make you a bad or unworthy person.

4. **Make Amends, if Possible**: If your actions hurt others, seek to make amends. Apologize and try to rectify the situation as best as you can. This can alleviate feelings of guilt and help restore a sense of personal integrity.

5. **Learn from the Experience**: Reflect on what led to the mistake and how you can avoid similar situations in the future. Use the experience as a learning opportunity for personal growth and development.

6. **Seek Support**: Sometimes, the burden of self-unforgiveness can be too heavy to bear alone. Do not hesitate to seek support from friends, family, or professionals who can provide guidance and perspective.

Self-forgiveness is not a one-time event but a process that might need to be revisited several times. It's about gradually shifting the narrative from one of self-condemnation to one of understanding, compassion, and growth. By forgiving oneself, individuals can break free from the cycle of guilt and shame, allowing them to move forward with greater self-awareness, empathy, and resilience. It is a vital step in healing not just oneself but also in fostering healthier relationships with others and leading a more fulfilling life.

CHAPTER 10

WHEN YOU NEED TO ASK FOR FORGIVENESS

We have talked about forgiving others, and forgiving self, but what about when it is your turn to ask for forgiveness? Asking for forgiveness can be a challenging endeavor for many individuals, even when they are aware of the emotional distress their actions have caused. The difficulty in seeking forgiveness often stems from a complex mix of psychological, emotional, and sometimes social factors. Understanding these can help in addressing the reluctance and moving towards making amends. Asking for forgiveness is a strength that lies in humility, there is power in sincerely asking for forgiveness.

The power and importance of asking for forgiveness lie in its ability to mend broken bonds, heal emotional wounds, and foster understanding and reconciliation. When someone takes the step to ask for forgiveness, they are acknowledging their responsibility for causing hurt or harm, which is a fundamental aspect of repairing trust and restoring relationships. This act is not just about expressing remorse; it is an offer to engage in a mutual healing process, demonstrating a willingness to understand the impact of one's actions and a commitment to do better in the future. Asking for forgiveness is a vulnerable, yet profoundly powerful gesture that can break down barriers of resentment and open up pathways to empathy and renewed connection.

I think it is important to mention that asking for forgiveness is also essential for one's moral and emotional development. It encourages individuals to engage in self-reflection, understand the consequences of their actions, and cultivate empathy for those they have hurt. This introspective process is vital for personal growth, as it transforms mistakes and wrongdoings into lessons and opportunities for improvement. It also relieves the individual of the heavy burden of guilt and shame, allowing them to move forward with a clearer conscience and a more positive self-image.

The process of asking for forgiveness also contributes to a more compassionate and forgiving culture. When individuals witness acts of genuine remorse and requests for forgiveness, it can inspire others to respond in kindness, fostering an environment where people are more understanding and supportive of each other's faults and failures. This cultural shift towards forgiveness and reconciliation can have far-reaching effects, promoting peace, cooperation, and a stronger sense of community. Thus, the act of asking for forgiveness is not only crucial for personal healing and relationship repair but also for building a more empathetic and kind-hearted society.

As children, our parents made us quickly ask for forgiveness when we were guilty of wrongdoing, what changed when we became adults? Here are a few reasons why it is hard for some people to ask for forgiveness, followed by advice for those struggling to apologize.

REASONS WHY ASKING FOR FORGIVENESS MIGHT BE HARD

1. **Pride and Ego**: Admitting wrongdoing can be a blow to one's ego. It requires acknowledging that one is not perfect and has

made mistakes. For some, this admission can be particularly difficult, leading to avoidance of the situation altogether.

2. **Fear of Rejection or Confrontation**: Some might fear that their apology will be rejected, or that it will lead to confrontation and further hurt. This fear can be paralyzing, preventing them from taking the necessary steps to seek forgiveness.

3. **Guilt and Shame**: While guilt can sometimes motivate individuals to seek forgiveness, it can also be overwhelming, leading to avoidance. The person might feel so ashamed of their actions that facing the person they hurt becomes incredibly daunting.

4. **Lack of Awareness or Understanding**: In some cases, individuals might not fully comprehend the impact of their actions or might not know how to appropriately express remorse. This lack of understanding can hinder their ability to seek forgiveness.

5. **Habitual Patterns or Psychological Barriers**: For some, not apologizing might be a pattern of behavior rooted in their upbringing or personal experiences. Psychological barriers, such as deep-seated issues of low self-worth or fear of vulnerability, can also make asking for forgiveness challenging.

ADVICE FOR THOSE STRUGGLING TO APOLOGIZE

1. **Reflect on the Impact**: Spend time reflecting on how your actions might have affected the other person. Try to understand the emotional distress caused from their perspective. This empathy can motivate you to seek forgiveness.

2. **Accept Responsibility**: Recognize that everyone makes mistakes, and owning up to yours is a sign of maturity and

strength. Accept responsibility for your actions without making excuses.

3. **Prepare for the Conversation**: If you are worried about how to express your apology, it can be helpful to prepare. Think about what you want to say, and perhaps write it down. Be clear about what you are apologizing for and express genuine remorse.

4. **Choose the Right Time and Place**: Look for an appropriate time and place to apologize, where you can have a calm and private conversation. Ensure that both you and the other person have the time and are in the right mindset for the conversation.

5. **Be Patient and Ready for Any Outcome**: Understand that the other person might need time to process your apology and that forgiveness might not be immediate. Be patient and respect their feelings and responses, even if it's not what you hoped for.

6. **Learn from the Experience**: Regardless of the outcome, use this as a learning experience. Reflect on what led to the situation and how you can prevent similar issues in the future. This reflection can lead to personal growth and better relationships moving forward.

7. **Seek Support**: If you are finding it particularly difficult to apologize, consider seeking support from a friend, family member, or professional who can provide guidance and perspective.

Asking for forgiveness is a courageous act that can lead to healed and restored relationships. It requires humility, empathy, and a genuine desire to make amends. By understanding the challenges and preparing oneself for the process, individuals can overcome the barriers to seeking forgiveness and take a significant step towards emotional reconciliation and growth.

Asking for forgiveness when you have hurt someone or a group of people is a fundamental step in the process of reconciliation and healing. It acknowledges the harm done, expresses remorse, and opens a path to restore trust and relationships. The act of seeking forgiveness is critical for both the person who caused the hurt and the one who was hurt. Here are several aspects that underscore the importance of asking for forgiveness:

1. Acknowledgment of Wrongdoing

Asking for forgiveness starts with acknowledging that you have done something wrong. This acknowledgment is crucial as it validates the feelings and experiences of the person or group who was hurt. It shows that you understand the impact of your actions and are willing to take responsibility for them. This can be a powerful step towards healing the hurt and rebuilding trust.

2. Expression of Remorse and Empathy

Seeking forgiveness typically involves expressing remorse for the harm caused. Genuine remorse shows that you not only understand the wrongness of your actions but also feel regret for the pain caused. It is an expression of empathy, reflecting that you can put yourself in the other person's shoes and appreciate the depth of their hurt.

3. Opportunity for Healing and Closure

Asking for forgiveness can provide an opportunity for healing and closure for both parties. For the one who was hurt, hearing an apology and seeing the willingness to make amends can be a crucial step in their healing process. It can help them move past the hurt and towards forgiveness. For the one who caused the harm, seeking forgiveness allows them to alleviate their guilt and take active steps toward becoming a better person.

4. Restoring Relationships

Hurt and grievances can cause rifts in relationships, sometimes leading to long-term estrangement or bitterness. Asking for forgiveness is an essential step in restoring these relationships. It opens up dialogue and shows a willingness to work through the issues, paving the way for reconciliation and rebuilding trust.

5. Personal Growth and Learning

Asking for forgiveness is also an opportunity for personal growth and learning. It requires humility and courage to admit wrong and face the consequences of one's actions. This process can lead to a deeper understanding of oneself, a more profound respect for others, and a commitment to change harmful behaviors or patterns.

6. Moral and Ethical Responsibility

From a moral and ethical standpoint, seeking forgiveness is the right thing to do when you have caused harm. It's a demonstration of integrity and a commitment to justice and fairness. It shows that you value the well-being and dignity of those you've hurt and are willing to take steps to right the wrong.

7. Promoting a Culture of Forgiveness and Compassion

On a broader scale, when individuals take responsibility for their actions and seek forgiveness, they contribute to a culture of forgiveness and compassion. Such a culture encourages openness, understanding, and a willingness to work through conflicts constructively. It sets a positive example for others and helps to create a more empathetic and forgiving community. We need this in our society as many no longer ask for forgiveness nor admit their wrong. Forgiveness or Unforgiveness can shift an entire culture even a nation that walks in unforgiveness.

Think about this for a moment. Imagine if we started a forgiveness movement across our nation, what might it look like in a year? Asking for forgiveness is not always easy; it can be a humbling and vulnerable experience. However, its importance cannot be overstated. It is a powerful act that can heal wounds, restore relationships, promote personal growth, and contribute to a more compassionate world. Whether in personal relationships, within communities, or in broader societal contexts, seeking forgiveness is a crucial step toward healing and harmony.

CHAPTER 11

LET'S BEGIN
THE FORGIVENESS PROCESS

alking out the process of forgiving others and oneself is a profound journey towards emotional liberation and personal growth cannot be reiterated enough. It is a proactive step toward healing emotional wounds and reclaiming control over one's emotional well-being. While this journey is deeply personal and some may navigate it independently, it is essential to recognize that the path is not always straightforward and can sometimes be laden with complex emotions and psychological barriers. Again, it is okay to seek support from friends or family members who can offer empathy, perspective, and encouragement. Their support can be invaluable in providing a sounding board and additional strength as you work through difficult emotions and situations.

However, for some, the wounds might be too deep, or the process too overwhelming to manage alone, especially if the hurt involves trauma, long-standing issues, or significantly impacts mental health. In such cases, seeking the help of a mental health professional is a sign of strength, not weakness. Licensed Professional mental health counselors or therapists are trained to guide individuals through the forgiveness process, providing a structured approach, coping strategies, and a safe, non-judgmental space to explore and heal from the pain. Remember, walking through the process of forgiveness can be a clinical issue that requires professional support and there is absolutely no shame in reaching out for help. Engaging with a mental health professional can significantly enhance the journey, ensuring that you do not have to walk the path alone and leading to a more effective and lasting healing. The decision to seek support is a testament to your commitment to your mental and emotional health and a courageous step towards a happier, more peaceful life.

Now that you have read the previous chapters, and you have not just gained knowledge but understanding; below is a structured approach that can help guide the forgiveness process. Here are steps that you can take to facilitate personal healing and forgiveness:

INSTRUCTIONS FOR FORGIVING OTHERS OR SELF:

1. **Find a Quiet Space**: Choose a quiet and comfortable place where you can be alone with your thoughts.
2. **Allow Yourself to Feel**: As you write, allow yourself to feel whatever emotions arise. Do not censor yourself; this process is personal and just for you unless you choose to share.
3. **Be Honest and Direct**: Express all that you have been holding back. This might include hurt, anger, disappointment, or confusion. Write down all of your emotions, they are normal reactions to what you have been through. Use previous chapters to assist you.
4. **Take Your Time**: Do not rush through the process. You might find it takes several attempts or sessions to say all you want to say. Make sure you set aside time where you won't be disrupted or distracted. It is important to choose a time when you are the most focused.

5. **Closure**: Remember everything is a choice. You get to choose at every stage. You are in control.

STEP 1: ACKNOWLEDGE YOUR FEELINGS

1. **Recognize and Name Your Emotions**: Understand and acknowledge the range of emotions you are feeling due to the hurt. This may include anger, sadness, betrayal, or disappointment. Admitting these feelings to yourself is the first step towards healing.

2. **Journaling**: Write down your thoughts and feelings about the offense and how it has affected your life. Be as detailed and honest as possible. This can help in externalizing your emotions and seeing them more clearly.

STEP 2: UNDERSTAND THE IMPACT

1. **Reflect on the Effects**: Consider how holding onto unforgiveness is impacting your life. How is it affecting your mental health, physical health, relationships, and overall well-being?

2. **Educate Yourself**: Learn about the benefits of forgiveness and the risks of unforgiveness. Understanding these can motivate you to embark on the journey of healing.

STEP 3: DECIDE TO FORGIVE

1. **Make a Commitment**: Forgiveness is a choice. It is important to consciously decide that you want to forgive, not for the sake of the offender, but for your own peace and freedom.

2. **Set Realistic Expectations**: Understand that forgiveness is a process and doesn't mean forgetting or condoning what happened. It is about letting go of the hold that the hurt has on you. Make a conscious choice to forgive.

STEP 4: WORK ON LETTING GO

1. **Challenge Negative Thoughts**: When you find yourself dwelling on the hurt or feeling resentful, challenge these thoughts. Ask yourself if they are beneficial or if they are keeping you tied to the past.

2. **Write a Letter**: Example letters are in the Appendix.

3. **Practice Mindfulness**: Engage in mindfulness exercises to stay present and reduce rumination. Techniques like deep breathing, meditation, or yoga can help calm your mind and reduce the emotional intensity associated with unforgiveness.

STEP 5: CULTIVATE EMPATHY AND UNDERSTANDING

1. **Try to Understand the Offender**: This does not mean excusing their actions, but rather trying to see the situation from their perspective. Consider what might have led them to act the way they did.

2. **Empathize with Yourself**: Be kind and compassionate towards yourself. Acknowledge your hurt and the strength it takes to move toward forgiveness.

STEP 6: SEEK RESOLUTION

1. **Express Your Feelings**: If possible and in a healthy way, express your feelings to the person who hurt you. This could be through a letter, a conversation, or another form of communication. If direct communication is not possible or healthy, consider writing a letter that you don't send. You don't need to send a written letter to receive healing, simply writing it is powerful as it allows you to share your thoughts, feelings, and emotions.

2. **Visualize Forgiveness**: Use visualization techniques to imagine forgiving the person who hurt you. Picture yourself letting go of the grudge and the relief that comes with it.

STEP 7: REBUILD AND MOVE FORWARD

1. **Reconnect with Positives**: Engage in activities that bring you joy and connect you with others. Rebuilding your life with positive experiences can diminish the space unforgiveness occupies in your mind.

2. **Set New Goals**: Focus on the future by setting new, personal goals. This can help shift your attention from the past to what you can control and look forward to.

STEP 8: MAINTAIN FORGIVENESS

1. **Practice Gratitude**: Regularly acknowledge things you are grateful for. Gratitude can shift your focus from what is wrong to what's right in your life.

2. **Continue Learning and Growing**: Recognize that setbacks may occur and that's okay. Forgiveness is a journey. Continue to learn about yourself and grow from your experiences.

By following these steps, individuals can actively work towards healing the wounds of unforgiveness and moving towards a more peaceful and fulfilling life.

Remember: It is important to remember that everyone's journey is unique, and progress takes time and patience. Do not try to work through all the steps in one day, pace yourself to ensure healing occurs. You may stay in some steps longer than others, but that's okay- it's your journey. If the process becomes overwhelming, consider seeking support from trusted friends, family, or a professional therapist.

CHAPTER 12

CLINICIANS WORKING WITH UNFORGIVENESS

A ddressing unforgiveness is a critical aspect of mental health care, given its far-reaching implications for psychological, physical, and relational well-being. Mental health professionals play a vital role in guiding clients through the complex emotional landscape of unforgiveness, helping them understand its roots, manifestations, and ways to overcome it. Here is a brief comprehensive overview of working with clients who harbor unforgiveness, underscored by evidence-based research and practices.

It is important to understand the impact of unforgiveness on mental health. Unforgiveness is often associated with increased anxiety, depression, and hostility, as well as diminished life satisfaction and well-being.[1] Clients holding onto unforgiveness may present with a range of symptoms, including persistent negative rumination, feelings of bitterness, and a pervasive sense of injustice. These mental health issues are not just limited to the emotional realm; they can manifest physically. Research has shown that unforgiveness is linked

---

1 Loren L. Toussaint, Everett L. Worthington, and David R. Williams, "Introduction: Context, Overview, and Guiding Questions," *Forgiveness and Health* (2015): 1-9, accessed 2024, doi: 10.1007/978-94-017-9993-5_1.

to increased heart rate, blood pressure, and stress response, which can contribute to a host of health issues.[2] It is crucial for mental health professionals to recognize these symptoms and understand the underlying unforgiveness that may be contributing to the client's distress.

In terms of relational issues, unforgiveness can lead to a breakdown in personal and social relationships, creating patterns of isolation, mistrust, and conflict.[3] The therapeutic process should, therefore, include an exploration of these interpersonal dynamics, helping clients see the impact of unforgiveness on their relationships and social life. This understanding can be a powerful motivator for clients to engage in the forgiveness process, as they begin to recognize the benefits of healing and reconciliation, not just for themselves but for their loved ones and community.

Working through unforgiveness often involves a multifaceted approach. Cognitive-behavioral strategies can help clients reframe their thoughts and beliefs about the offense and offender, reducing the emotional hold on unforgiveness.[4] Additionally, empathy exercises and forgiveness interventions can facilitate a shift from resentment to understanding and compassion. It's also important to address any underlying trauma or psychological issues that may be intertwined with the unforgiveness, ensuring a holistic approach to healing.

---

2 Britta A. Larsen et al., "The Immediate and Delayed Cardiovascular Benefits of Forgiving," *Psychosomatic Medicine* 74, no. 7 (2012): 745-750, accessed 2024, doi: 10.1097/psy.0b013e31825fe96c.

3 Everett Worthington, Jr., *Moving Forward: Six steps to forgiving yourself and breaking free from the past* (WaterBrook, 2013).

4 Nathaniel G. Wade et al., "Efficacy of Psychotherapeutic Interventions to Promote Forgiveness: A Meta-Analysis.," *Journal of Consulting and Clinical Psychology* 82, no. 1 (2014): 154-170, accessed 2024, doi: 10.1037/a0035268.

Mental health professionals should be aware of the cultural, spiritual, and individual factors that influence the forgiveness process. What constitutes forgiveness and the path to achieving it can vary significantly among individuals, and it's important to respect these differences. The therapeutic approach should be tailored to fit the client's cultural background, personal beliefs, and specific circumstances, creating a supportive and effective framework for healing and growth. Cultural and religious awareness is paramount in ensuring a respectful, empathetic, and effective therapeutic process, particularly when navigating sensitive issues such as unforgiveness. Professionals must recognize and honor the diverse cultural and religious backgrounds of their clients, understanding that these factors significantly influence perceptions of forgiveness, interpersonal relationships, and healing practices. Therapists should be well-versed in cultural competency, actively seeking to understand the client's cultural and religious context, asking open-ended questions, and showing genuine interest and respect for their beliefs and values.

Doing no harm, a fundamental principle in all therapeutic practices, is especially critical when dealing with the deeply personal and often painful journey towards forgiveness. Mental health professionals must approach the topic with sensitivity and care, avoiding any imposition of personal beliefs or biases. They should provide a supportive and non-judgmental space where clients can explore their feelings and beliefs about forgiveness at their own pace. Therapists must also be vigilant about the potential for re-traumatization or increased distress that discussions around forgiveness might evoke and be prepared to provide appropriate support and referrals if needed. By prioritizing cultural and religious awareness and adhering to the principle of doing no harm, mental health professionals can ensure that their approach to unforgiveness is both respectful and healing, fostering a therapeutic environment where clients feel understood, valued, and empowered to navigate their path towards emotional well-being.

I believe it was important to write this section for mental health professionals who are emerging in the profession and as a reminder to others that unforgiveness is a critical component of mental health care, with significant implications for psychological, physical, and relational health. Mental health professionals must be equipped to recognize and understand unforgiveness, employing evidence-based strategies and a culturally sensitive approach to guide clients through the healing process. By helping clients release the burden of unforgiveness, therapists can facilitate a journey toward greater emotional freedom, health, and interpersonal harmony.

A FEW EXAMPLES OF WORK THAT CAN BE DONE:

FOR CLINICIANS: Cognitive Behavioral Therapy (CBT) is a practical, hands-on approach that can be particularly effective in helping clients work through the process of forgiveness. It focuses on identifying and changing unhelpful patterns of thinking and behavior. Here are steps and processes using CBT techniques that can guide clients on their journey to forgiveness:

STEP 1: IDENTIFYING AND UNDERSTANDING EMOTIONS

1. **Emotional Awareness**: Clients are encouraged to express and acknowledge all the emotions related to the hurt and betrayal they have experienced. This may include anger, sadness, betrayal, or fear. Validating these emotions is crucial in the forgiveness process.

2. **Linking Thoughts and Emotions**: Clients learn to identify specific thoughts that trigger emotional responses. For instance,

a thought like "I will never be able to trust anyone again" might lead to feelings of despair or bitterness.

STEP 2: CHALLENGING UNHELPFUL THOUGHTS

1. **Cognitive Restructuring**: Clients are guided to challenge and reframe irrational or unhelpful thoughts that hinder the forgiveness process. This involves questioning the evidence for these thoughts, exploring alternative viewpoints, and developing more balanced and constructive thinking patterns.

2. **Developing Empathy**: Part of changing thought patterns could include trying to understand the situation from the perspective of the person who caused the harm. It's okay for a client not to gain an understanding as to why the pain or trauma occurred, especially in unique circumstances. Seeking to gain understanding, doesn't excuse their offenders' behavior but can reduce the personalization and intensity of the negative emotions.

STEP 3: BUILDING FORGIVENESS SKILLS

1. **Perspective Taking**: Clients may be encouraged depending on the type of offense to consider a broader perspective, looking at the situation in a more detached and objective way. This might involve considering the circumstances that led to the person's harmful actions or contemplating the imperfections in every individual. This will not be in all cases.

2. **Empathy and Compassion Development**: Clients practice empathy and compassion, first towards themselves and then towards others.

   This includes forgiving themselves for any negative feelings and acknowledging that everyone is capable of making mistakes.

STEP 4: REDUCING AVOIDANCE AND INCREASING ACCEPTANCE

1. **Acceptance**: Clients work on accepting what happened as a part of their past, acknowledging that while it cannot be changed, they can change their response for their healing. Acceptance is a crucial step in reducing the emotional power of past events.

2. **Behavioral Activation**: Clients are encouraged to engage in positive activities and relationships. Some clients will isolate because of hurt and disappointment and for fear of being hurt again. Practicing positive interaction can help in creating new, positive experiences and associations.

STEP 5: REHEARSING FORGIVENESS AND APPLYING IT IN REAL LIFE

1. **Role Playing**: Through role-playing exercises, clients can practice how they might forgive in real life. This can include writing a letter of forgiveness (not necessarily to be sent) or imagining a conversation where they express forgiveness.

2. **Gradual Exposure**: Clients may be encouraged to gradually expose themselves to thoughts of the person or situations related to the hurtful event while using the new coping skills they've learned to manage their emotional responses.

STEP 6: CONSOLIDATING GAINS AND PLANNING FOR THE FUTURE

1. **Relapse Prevention**: Clients learn strategies to maintain their new forgiveness perspective and cope with potential future hurts or reminders of past hurts. This includes planning for how to deal with negative emotions and thoughts if they arise.

2. **Continued Practice**: Forgiveness is seen as an ongoing practice rather than a one-time event. Clients are encouraged to continue practicing forgiveness in various aspects of their lives, reinforcing the skills and perspectives they have learned.

Throughout these steps, the therapist provides support, guidance, and feedback, helping the client to navigate the complex emotions and thoughts that accompany the forgiveness process. It is important to note that forgiveness is a personal journey and can vary greatly from one individual to another. The pace and specific techniques used should be tailored to each client's unique situation and needs. With patience and persistence, CBT can provide a structured path toward healing and forgiveness.

Please note: The empathy exercises are generally not recommended for use with individuals who have experienced sexual assault, domestic violence, or child abuse. These situations involve profound trauma and power imbalances that can make attempts at empathy for the perpetrator inappropriate and potentially retraumatizing. In cases of severe abuse, the primary focus should be on the safety, empowerment, and healing of the survivor. Mental health professionals must approach such cases with extreme care, sensitivity, and adherence to trauma-informed care principles. If you or someone you know is dealing with the aftermath of sexual assault, domestic violence, or child abuse, please seek support from a qualified professional who specializes in trauma and can provide the appropriate care and guidance. Always prioritize the safety and well-being of the survivor in these situations.

Reframing is a cognitive behavioral technique that helps individuals look at situations from a different perspective. It can be particularly effective in helping clients address negative thoughts, feelings, and beliefs that contribute to unforgiveness. Here are 1-2 reframing exercises mental health professionals might facilitate:

1. **Reframing Negative Beliefs**: In this exercise, the client is first asked to express a negative belief related to the person or situation they cannot forgive, such as "They hurt me because

they think I'm worthless." The therapist then guides the client in challenging this belief and considering alternative, more balanced thoughts. For instance, the therapist might ask, "What evidence supports this belief? What evidence contradicts it? Could there be another reason they acted this way that does not reflect on your worth as a person?" Through this dialogue, the client learns to identify and dispute negative beliefs, replacing them with thoughts that are more objective and less harmful. The aim is to shift the client's perspective from one that is self-critical and fixed to one that is more understanding and flexible.

2. **Positive Outcome Reframing**: In this exercise, the client is asked to think about a situation where they felt wronged and focus on the negative emotions and outcomes. The therapist then encourages the client to reframe the situation by identifying any positive outcomes or learning experiences that emerged from it. For example, if a client is struggling to forgive a betrayal by a friend, the therapist might guide them to consider how the situation might have led to personal growth, a stronger sense of self, or the realization of who their true friends are. This reframing exercise helps the client to acknowledge the pain while also recognizing that even negative experiences can contribute to positive personal development. It shifts the focus from what was lost to what might have been gained or learned.

In using these reframing exercises, therapists need to proceed with sensitivity and validation of the client's feelings. The goal is not to diminish the hurt or wrongdoing but to help the client view their experiences in a way that reduces emotional distress and opens up possibilities for healing and forgiveness.

CHAPTER 13

RELIGIOUS TRAUMA AND UNFORGIVENESS

FORGIVING IN THE CHURCH IS STILL A PROCESS

Religious Trauma in many communities of faith is a particularly profound form of emotional and spiritual trauma because it occurs in a place that is meant to be a sanctuary of love, acceptance, and community. Religious groups are often viewed by their believers as a representation of divine love and grace in the world, a gathering of individuals united under the common purpose of worship and spiritual growth. When the trust inherent in this sacred community is broken, it can lead to deep, lasting pain that is difficult to reconcile and overcome.

Religious Trauma, sometimes referred to as "Church hurt" or "Religious hurt," holds a unique place in the discussion of emotional and spiritual trauma, particularly within the Christian community. It's important to note that while religious trauma can occur across various religious groups or affiliations and does, my focus here is specifically on the Christian community. This focus stems from my personal background and extensive work within Christian community circles, dealing with issues related to trauma, transgenerational trauma, and religious trauma. My connection to this community allows for a nuanced understanding of the specific challenges and cultural dynamics at play within Christian contexts.

The Christian church, like many religious institutions, has been on a journey of recognizing and integrating professional mental health counseling into its care structures. While there has been significant progress, there remains a gap in fully embracing and understanding the importance of licensed professional counseling alongside pastoral care. It's not uncommon for some within the community to rely solely on pastoral counseling. While pastoral care is invaluable, it is crucial to recognize the distinction between pastoral counseling and professional licensed counseling, particularly when addressing complex mental health issues. This is not a critique of pastoral counseling but an acknowledgment of the specialized training and expertise that licensed professionals bring to the table, especially for mental health disorders that are deeply impacting one's soul and well-being.

Incorporating professional mental health practitioners is not just a complementary approach; it is a necessary integration for addressing the multifaceted nature of religious trauma. The Christian church often uses terms like "church hurt," but regardless of the nomenclature, the impact is profound and often debilitating. Such trauma, though frequently minimized or misunderstood, requires the insight and intervention of those trained to navigate the complexities of psychological and emotional healing. As we continue to work within the Christian community, it is essential to advocate for and support a collaborative approach that brings together spiritual care and professional counseling, ensuring that those suffering from all hurt receive comprehensive, empathetic, and effective care. This commitment to healing is not just about addressing individual wounds;

it is about fostering a healthier, more resilient community that reflects the love, grace, and compassion at the heart of the Christian faith.

Mental Health Professionals can play a crucial role in addressing the uniqueness of religious trauma by providing a safe, non-judgmental space for individuals to explore and heal from their spiritual and emotional wounds, offering a blend of professional psychological insight with a sensitive understanding of religious context. Their expertise allows them to navigate the complex interplay between faith, identity, and trauma, facilitating a healing journey that respects both the individual's spiritual and mental health needs. The complex interplay often lies at unforgiveness, which can become a mental health or clinical issue. Here is a look at the uniqueness of religious trauma or church hurt and how scripture from the Bible (King James Version) can provide insight and guidance for healing and forgiveness:

THE UNIQUENESS OF RELIGIOUS TRAUMA OR "CHURCH HURT"

1. **Betrayal of Trust**: The church is often seen as a refuge from the harshness of the world, a place where individuals can be vulnerable and find unconditional support. When leaders or members of the church act in ways that are hurtful, manipulative, or abusive, it violates this sacred trust, making the hurt feel like a betrayal by God's representatives.

2. **Spiritual Disillusionment**: Church or religious hurt can lead to questions and doubts about one's faith and beliefs. When those who are supposed to embody Christian principles act contrary to them, it can shake the foundation of what individuals believe and their relationship with God.

3. **Community Alienation**: Being hurt by the church or religious affiliation can lead to feelings of isolation and alienation from the community that was once a significant source of friendship

and support. This loss of community can intensify the pain and make the healing process more challenging.

4. **Identity Crisis**: For many, their church or religious community and spiritual life are central to their identity. When hurt occurs within this context, it can lead to an identity crisis, leaving individuals unsure of who they are and where they belong.

SCRIPTURAL GUIDANCE AND SUPPORT

1. **Understanding Human Fallibility**: "For all have sinned and come short of the glory of God;" - Romans 3:23. This verse reminds us that all humans are fallible and capable of causing hurt, even within the church. Recognizing this can help in processing the hurt from a perspective of human imperfection.

2. **The Call to Forgive**: "Then came Peter to him, and said, Lord, how oft shall my brother sin against me, and I forgive him? till seven times? Jesus saith unto him, I say not unto thee, Until seven times: but, Until seventy times seven." - Matthew 18:21-22. This passage emphasizes the importance of forgiveness, not as a one-time act but as a continual process, which is especially pertinent in overcoming church hurt.

3. **God's Comfort and Justice**: "Casting all your care upon him; for He careth for you." - 1 Peter 5:7. This verse encourages individuals to bring their pain and worries to God, trusting in His care and justice. It provides comfort, knowing that God is aware of the hurts, and is a source of healing. Comfort is not just a position for healing but a place (heavenly realm for empowerment).

4. **The Promise of Healing and Restoration**: "He healeth the broken in heart, and bindeth up their wounds." - Psalms 147:3. This verse offers hope for healing and restoration, affirming

that God is close to the brokenhearted and actively works to heal their wounds if you will work with Him.

5. **Love as the Highest Command**: "A new commandment I give unto you, That ye love one another; as I have loved you, that ye also love one another." - John 13:34. This commandment serves as a reminder of the fundamental principle of discipleship - love. Even in the face of hurt, adhering to this command can guide individuals toward healing and reconciliation when coupled with the principles taught in the writing on the previous pages. You can know scripture without having wisdom. Knowledge gives you the "what", "wisdom" gives you the "how" and understanding gives you the "why". *I Forgive You: Choosing Freedom Over Bondage* is God-inspired and aligns with His Holy Word.

The journey of healing from religious trauma is deeply personal and often complex, requiring time, understanding, and often guidance from trusted spiritual and/or professional counselors. Scripture can and does offer comfort and direction, but it is also important to seek support from a community or individuals who can assist someone process through the pain. By acknowledging the hurt, actively working towards forgiveness, and leaning on the principles of faith and love, individuals can find a path through the pain toward healing and renewed spiritual strength.

Disappointment from church or religious hurt, especially when it involves spiritual leaders, is a particularly profound and disorienting experience.

Spiritual leaders are often held in high regard, seen as moral and ethical guides, and are expected to be exemplary representatives of their faith's teachings and values. When these individuals cause hurt, whether through manipulation, abuse of power, moral failures, or negligence, it can shake the very foundations of a person's faith and Christian journey. Here are some aspects and impacts of disappointment stemming from spiritual leaders:

1. Broken Trust

The relationship between spiritual leaders and their congregations is built on a foundation of trust. People look up to these leaders for guidance and support, and to exemplify the teachings they preach. When leaders fail or hurt their members, it is not just viewed as a personal letdown; it is considered a break in a sacred trust. This betrayal can leave individuals questioning not only their relationship with the church but their spiritual beliefs as well.

2. Spiritual Disillusionment

For many, their spiritual leaders are not just religious figures but are pivotal in their spiritual journey and understanding of divine principles. When these leaders fall short, it can lead to spiritual disillusionment. Individuals may begin to question the validity of the teachings, the integrity of the institution, and even their faith and beliefs. This disillusionment can lead to a deep spiritual crisis, affecting their relationship with the divine God and their spiritual identity.

3. Emotional Turmoil and Isolation

The hurt or perceived hurt caused by spiritual leaders can evoke a complex mix of emotions: anger, confusion, sadness, and a profound sense of betrayal. Given the central role of religion in many people's lives, this emotional turmoil can be particularly intense and pervasive. Additionally, there may be a sense of isolation, especially if the community continues to support the leader or if the individual feels they cannot express their disillusionment without judgment.

4. Impact on Community and Relationships

Church or religious communities are often tight-knit and form a significant part of an individual's social support and identity. When leaders cause hurt, it can disrupt the entire church or religious community, creating divisions, conflicts, and sometimes forcing individuals to leave the church or religious community they once loved. The impact extends beyond individual spirituality, affecting friendships, family relationships, and one's sense of belonging.

5. Challenges in Rebuilding Faith

Recovering from spiritual hurt involves not just dealing with the personal emotional impact but often requires rebuilding one's faith and trust in the religious institution or finding a new path altogether. The disappointment can lead to wariness toward other spiritual leaders and communities, making it challenging to reconnect or find a new spiritual home. The former church member often goes from church to church seeking a safe place or they may stop going to church altogether because of disappointment.

The disappointment from church or religious hurt is deep and multifaceted, touching on every aspect of an individual's life. It is a breach of moral and ethical expectations that leaves lasting scars. Healing from such hurt requires time, reflection, often a reevaluation of one's beliefs and values, and sometimes the support of understanding individuals or professionals who can guide the healing process. Recognizing the pain, validating the experience, and taking steps towards personal healing is crucial for individuals affected by such disappointments.

For many, their religious identity is not just a belief they hold; it is a comprehensive way of life, informing their values, ethics, community, and understanding of the world. When the trust and safety of this fundamental part of their identity are compromised, especially by those expected to uphold it, the ramifications are profound and lasting.

DEEP AND MULTIFACETED IMPACT

1. **Moral and Ethical Disorientation**: Spiritual leaders are often seen as moral compasses. When they act in ways that are hurtful or unethical, it can create a sense of moral and ethical disorientation. Individuals may begin to question what is right and wrong, who they can trust, and the validity of moral authorities. This disorientation can affect decision-making, relationships, and personal ethics.

2. **Psychological Impact**: The psychological impact of religious or church hurt is significant. It can lead to depression, anxiety, and other mental health issues. The betrayal and disappointment can also lead to complex post-traumatic stress, especially if the hurt involves abuse or long-term manipulation. The scars left are not just emotional; they are psychological wounds that require time and often professional help to heal.

3. **Social and Relational Strain**: Religious communities are often central to social life and identity. When hurt occurs, individuals may feel they have to withdraw from these communities to protect themselves from further pain. This withdrawal can lead to isolation, loneliness, and the loss of important social support systems. Furthermore, if friends or family members remain part of the community or do not understand the individual's hurt, it can strain or sever these relationships.

4. **Spiritual Alienation**: Perhaps one of the most profound impacts is the sense of spiritual alienation. Individuals may feel abandoned by their faith or God's divine presence. They might struggle with unanswered prayers or unmet spiritual needs that they once believed their faith or community would support. This alienation can lead to a loss of spiritual direction and purpose, deeply affecting one's sense of self and place in the universe.

BREACH OF MORAL AND ETHICAL EXPECTATIONS

1. **Violation of Sacred Trust**: Religious and spiritual institutions are built on a foundation of sacred trust. This is not just trust in leaders but in the entire belief system and community. When leaders breach this trust, it is not just a personal failure; it is seen as a failure of the institution and sometimes the faith itself. This violation can leave individuals questioning not just the individuals involved but the very doctrines and practices they once held sacred.

2. **Lasting Scars of Hypocrisy**: One of the most stinging aspects of religious or church hurt is the perceived hypocrisy. Spiritual teachings often emphasize virtues like honesty, compassion, and integrity. When leaders act contrary to these teachings, it highlights a hypocrisy that can be deeply disillusioning. The lasting scar is not just the hurt itself but the cynicism and skepticism that replace previous sincerity and faith.

3. **Ethical Dilemmas and Confusion**: Those hurt by religious or church leaders often face ethical dilemmas and confusion. They might grapple with balancing forgiveness and accountability, justice and compassion. The ethical framework they once relied on for making such decisions is the same framework that has

been compromised, leaving them to navigate these complex issues without clear guidance.

The disappointment and hurt caused by church or religious institutions require a journey through grief, questioning, and rebuilding. It is about finding a way to heal the wounds while reevaluating and reconstructing one's spiritual, ethical, and social identity. For many, this journey involves forging a new relationship with their spirituality, one that is perhaps more personal, resilient, and informed by their experiences. It is a path marked by the search for understanding, healing, and ultimately, a renewed sense of peace and purpose.

In more recent years, there has been a greater increase or emergence of pastors or spiritual leaders being referenced as or now regarded as spiritual mothers and fathers, figures who provide guidance, nurture, and protection to their congregation. This practice was not as prevalent historically as it is today, where a large body of pastoral or spiritual leaders call their parishioners their spiritual sons and daughters. This relationship is not merely functional; it is deeply emotional and symbolic, representing a bond of trust, respect, and spiritual intimacy. When these revered figures cause hurt or perceived hurt, the impact can be particularly traumatic, leading to profound emotional wounds even more so if the individuals have unresolved trauma related to their natural or birth parents.

THE ROLE OF SPIRITUAL PARENTS IS SAID TO BE ONE OF:

1. **Guidance and Mentorship**: Spiritual parents are seen as guides on the journey of faith, offering wisdom, insight, and mentorship. They help interpret spiritual texts, provide moral and ethical guidance, and support individuals through life's challenges.

2. **Emotional and Spiritual Support**: Like parental figures, spiritual leaders are often expected to provide emotional and spiritual support. They are often the first point of contact in times of crisis, grief, or moral dilemma. The relationship is built on a deep level of emotional and spiritual trust.

3. **Role Models**: Spiritual mothers and fathers are also perceived as role models, embodying the ideals and values of the faith. Their lives and actions are often seen as direct representations of their teachings and of the faith they profess.

THE HURT FROM SPIRITUAL PARENTS

1. **Breach of Sacred Trust**: When spiritual leaders, viewed as spiritual parents, cause hurt, it is perceived as a profound breach of sacred trust. This betrayal can feel more personal and impactful than other types of hurt because of the deep emotional and spiritual ties involved. The congregation might have shared their deepest fears, sins, and hopes with their spiritual leaders, making any betrayal or hurt deeply wounding.

2. **Confusion and Doubt**: The hurt can lead to confusion and doubt about one's faith and beliefs. Individuals may question the validity of the teachings, the sincerity of the faith community, and their personal spiritual experiences. If the spiritual parent has been a significant figure in the individual's spiritual development, this can lead to a reevaluation of their entire spiritual journey.

3. **Emotional Turmoil**: The emotional turmoil resulting from such betrayal can be intense. It may include feelings of anger, betrayal, depression, and loneliness. Because the relationship with a spiritual parent is so profound, that the emotional wounds

can be deep, sometimes leading to a sense of abandonment or spiritual orphanhood.

THE LEVEL OF TRAUMA AND EMOTIONAL WOUNDS

1. **Trauma**: The trauma from spiritual hurt can be severe, particularly if it involves abuse, manipulation, or significant betrayal. The sense of safety and sanctity that is expected in spiritual relationships is shattered, leaving individuals to grapple with the aftermath in their emotional and spiritual lives.

2. **Long-lasting Emotional Wounds**: The emotional wounds from such hurt are often long-lasting. They can affect future relationships, the ability to trust spiritual leaders, and the willingness to engage with religious communities. The hurt can also lead to long-term spiritual struggles or crises of faith.

3. **Identity Crisis**: Given that faith and spiritual community often form a significant part of an individual's identity, hurt from spiritual parents can lead to an identity crisis. Individuals may feel lost, unsure about who they are, and disconnected from their spiritual roots.

4. **Need for Comprehensive Healing**: Healing from this type of hurt typically requires a comprehensive approach, addressing not just the emotional and psychological aspects but also the spiritual dimensions. It might involve seeking support from trusted friends, family, or Licensed Mental Health Professionals who understand the unique nature of spiritual hurt. It also often involves a process of redefining one's faith and spirituality in a way that acknowledges the hurt but also allows for personal growth and healing.

When individuals view their pastors or spiritual leaders as spiritual mothers and fathers, the potential for deep emotional and spiritual hurt is significant if those leaders fail or cause harm or perceived harm. Understanding the nature of this relationship and the level of trust involved is crucial in acknowledging the depth of the hurt and the complex journey of healing that follows.

Licensed Mental Health Professional (Psychologist, LCSWs, LPCs) Counseling can be a vital resource for Christians or any faith community suffering from hurt and unforgiveness, especially when the source of the pain is a trusted spiritual leader. Both scripture and psychological science offer robust frameworks for understanding and healing from such deep emotional and spiritual wounds. Unfortunately, sometimes the religious community struggles with seeking professional support believing as long as they pray and the individual believes for healing, the issue should be resolved.

Licensed Mental Health Professionals can be an invaluable asset when dealing with this type of hurt and the unforgiveness that often comes with it, particularly when these feelings stem from deep-seated emotional and spiritual wounds. While prayer and spiritual practices are vital components of healing, the addition of professional counseling offers a complementary path to recovery, one that integrates spiritual beliefs with psychological expertise.

It is essential to recognize that emotional and psychological pain are aspects of the human experience that can benefit from specialized intervention, just like physical ailments. Licensed Mental Health Professionals are trained to understand the complexities of the human mind and emotions, providing strategies and support that facilitate healing and growth. They offer a safe, confidential space to explore deeply personal and painful experiences, working with individuals to unravel the threads of their hurt, understand their reactions, and develop healthier coping mechanisms. This professional guidance is particularly crucial when the source of pain is a trusted spiritual leader, as the betrayal can leave individuals feeling isolated, confused, and spiritually adrift.

Integrating scripture and psychological science can provide a holistic approach to healing. Many Licensed Mental Health Professionals who work with religious communities are not only well-versed in psychological theory but also sensitive to the spiritual dimensions of healing. They can help individuals reconcile their emotional and spiritual struggles, using a framework that respects and incorporates their faith values. This approach can be reassuring for Christians who may fear that seeking professional help might lead them away from their spiritual beliefs. On the contrary, when done thoughtfully, counseling can deepen one's faith, offering insights and understandings that enrich one's spiritual life.

Addressing the stigma surrounding professional counseling in religious communities is also crucial. It is important to challenge the notion that professional help signifies a lack of faith or spiritual failure. Just as visiting a doctor for a physical illness is seen as both sensible and necessary, seeking a counselor for emotional and psychological distress should be viewed in the same light. Faith leaders and community members can play a significant role in breaking down these barriers, openly discussing the benefits of counseling, sharing personal experiences of healing, and providing support and resources for those seeking help.

Licensed Professional Counseling does not replace prayer or spiritual support; rather, it complements and enhances these spiritual practices. It offers a bridge between the emotional and spiritual aspects of healing, providing tools and insights that facilitate a more profound and lasting recovery. For Christians struggling with hurt and unforgiveness, especially from deep wounds inflicted within a religious context, professional counseling can be a powerful ally on the journey toward healing, wholeness, and renewed faith. By embracing this resource, individuals and communities can move towards a more integrated and holistic approach to healing, one that honors both the psychological and spiritual dimensions of their being.

Here's how counseling, informed by both these domains, can aid in the healing process:

SCRIPTURAL FOUNDATIONS FOR COUNSELING

1. **Encouragement to Seek Help**: Scripture encourages seeking guidance and support. Proverbs 11:14 says, "Where no counsel is, the people fall: but in the multitude of counsellors there is safety." This verse suggests that seeking counsel is not only wise but provides safety and support, an important reminder for those hesitant to seek help.

2. **The Role of Forgiveness**: Ephesians 4:31-32 states, "Let all bitterness, and wrath, and anger, and clamour, and evil speaking, be put away from you, with all malice: And be ye kind one to another, tenderhearted, forgiving one another, even as God for Christ's sake hath forgiven you." Counseling can help individuals understand and apply the process of forgiveness, not as an immediate act, but as a journey towards emotional and spiritual healing.

3. **Healing and Restoration**: Psalms 147:3, "He healeth the broken in heart, and bindeth up their wounds," speaks to God's role in healing. Counseling can serve as a means through which individuals understand and experience this healing, integrating their spiritual beliefs with psychological healing processes.

SCIENTIFIC AND THERAPEUTIC APPROACHES

1. **Understanding the Impact of Trauma**: Psychological science recognizes the profound impact of spiritual trauma and the complex dynamics of religious communities. Counseling provides a safe space to explore these impacts, understand the nature of spiritual trauma, and work through the emotions and doubts that arise from such experiences.

2. **Cognitive Behavioral Therapy (CBT)**: CBT can be particularly effective in helping individuals address the negative thought patterns and beliefs that stem from church hurt. It helps in restructuring these thoughts and finding more constructive ways to deal with emotions and forgiveness. Licensed.

3. **Narrative Therapy**: This approach can help individuals reframe their personal stories, allowing them to separate their identity from the hurt and regain a sense of agency and purpose. It's particularly useful in reconstructing one's spiritual narrative.

4. **Group Therapy or Support Groups**: Being part of a therapy group with others who have experienced similar hurts can provide a sense of community and understanding that is often lost when one leaves or feels betrayed by their religious community.

INTEGRATED APPROACH FOR COMPREHENSIVE HEALING

1. **Combining Scripture with Therapy**: An integrated approach that respects and incorporates an individual's faith can be particularly comforting and effective. It allows individuals to see their journey of healing as part of their spiritual walk, with scriptural wisdom guiding and complementing the psychological healing process.

2. **Encouragement Towards Forgiveness and Reconciliation**: Counseling can help individuals explore forgiveness in a healthy and gradual way, acknowledging the pain and the time it takes to genuinely forgive. For some, this may eventually lead to reconciliation, while for others, it may mean finding peace without reconciliation. Ephesians 4:32 says, "And be ye kind one to another, tenderhearted, forgiving one another, even as God for Christ's sake hath forgiven you".

3. **Fostering Spiritual Growth and Reflection**: Counseling can encourage individuals to reflect on their spiritual beliefs and experiences, fostering a mature and perhaps transformed faith that incorporates their experiences, questions, and growth. Romans 12: says, "And be not conformed to this world: but be ye transformed by the renewing of your mind, that ye may prove what is that good, and acceptable, and perfect, will of God" which aligns with this integrative approach.

4. **Providing Tools and Strategies**: Counseling offers practical tools and strategies for dealing with the emotional, psychological, and sometimes physical manifestations of church hurt. This includes stress management techniques, coping strategies for managing triggers, and ways to rebuild trust in relationships.

Counseling offers a multi-dimensional approach to healing from religious trauma or church hurt and unforgiveness, integrating spiritual, emotional, and psychological aspects. It respects the unique pain and challenges faced by individuals in these situations while providing a structured path toward healing, empowerment, and renewed faith. For Christians navigating the aftermath of spiritual betrayal or community hurt, counseling can be a crucial step toward reclaiming their spiritual path and overall well-being.

Cognitive Behavioral Therapy (CBT) is a widely used form of psychotherapy that focuses on identifying and changing negative or inaccurate thinking patterns, emotional responses, and behaviors. It is grounded in the concept that our thoughts, feelings, and behaviors are interconnected, and that changing negative thought patterns can lead to changes in feelings and behaviors. CBT is known for being short-term and goal-oriented, providing individuals with tools and strategies they can use to cope with and overcome challenges.

TECHNIQUES OF CBT

1. **Cognitive Restructuring or Reframing**: This involves identifying and challenging negative or harmful thoughts. The counselor helps the client recognize their pattern of negative thinking and teaches them to challenge these thoughts and replace them with more balanced and realistic ones.

2. **Behavioral Activation**: This technique is used to help individuals engage more in activities they enjoy or find meaningful. It is especially useful in cases of depression where inaction or withdrawal is prominent. Behavioral activation helps to break the cycle of inactivity and negative moods.

3. **Exposure Therapy**: Often used for treating anxiety disorders, exposure therapy involves gradually exposing clients to feared objects or situations in a controlled and safe manner. This helps reduce fear and anxiety responses over time.

4. **Activity Scheduling and Planning**: Clients learn to schedule activities that can improve their mood and break patterns of avoidance or procrastination. This technique encourages active engagement in life and can help increase feelings of efficacy and satisfaction.

5. **Mindfulness and Relaxation Techniques**: While not traditional CBT techniques, many modern CBT approaches

incorporate mindfulness and relaxation to help clients focus on the present moment and reduce anxiety. These techniques can also help with emotional regulation.

INTEGRATING CBT TECHNIQUES INTO COUNSELING

Counselors can integrate CBT techniques into their practice in various ways, depending on the individual client's needs and contexts. Here are some examples:

1. **Integrating Cognitive Restructuring with Scriptural Truths**: For Christian clients, counselors might integrate cognitive restructuring with scriptural truths. For example, if a client is struggling with feelings of worthlessness, a counselor might help them challenge this thought with personal affirmations grounded in their faith, such as the inherent worth and love bestowed upon them as a creation of God (e.g., Psalms 139:14).

2. **Behavioral Activation through Service or Community Engagement**: A counselor might encourage a client to engage in church or community service as a form of behavioral activation. Such engagement not only gets the client active and involved in meaningful work but also helps reconnect them with a community, fostering a sense of belonging and purpose.

3. **Exposure Therapy for Religious Trauma**: If a client is dealing with anxiety stemming from a specific religious trauma, such as fear of attending church, a counselor might use graded exposure techniques to help them slowly and systematically face their fear in manageable steps, possibly integrating prayer or meditation as calming practices during the exposure.

4. **Activity Scheduling Around Spiritual Practices**: Counselors might help clients schedule regular spiritual practices such as prayer, meditation, or scripture study into their daily routine.

This can provide structure and reinforce positive, reflective personal time, which can improve mood and provide a sense of stability. As an example, Joshua 1:8 says, "This book of the law shall not depart out of thy mouth; but thou shalt meditate therein day and night, that thou mayest observe to do according to all that is written therein: for then thou shalt make thy way prosperous, and then thou shalt have good success).

5. **Mindfulness and Prayer**: Integrating mindfulness with prayer can be powerful for clients dealing with anxiety or stress. Counselors can guide clients in mindfulness practices that allow them to be fully present during prayer or meditation, enhancing the spiritual and emotional benefits of these practices. Yes, mindfulness is scriptural, it is where it started. Philippians 4:8-9 says, "Finally, brethren, whatsoever things are true, whatsoever things are honest, whatsoever things are just, whatsoever things are pure, whatsoever things are lovely, whatsoever things are of good report; if there be any virtue, and if there be any praise, think on these things. 9Those things, which ye have both learned, and received, and heard, and seen in me, do: and the God of peace shall be with you.

By integrating these CBT techniques, mental health professionals can provide a robust framework that addresses the cognitive, behavioral, and emotional needs of their clients. For Christian clients or those dealing with religious hurt, these techniques can be tailored to respect and incorporate their faith, providing a holistic approach to healing and growth. As with all therapeutic interventions, the key is to work collaboratively with the client, tailoring the approach to their unique needs, and respecting their values and beliefs.

CLOSING REMARKS
BY DR. DONNA D. FERGUSON

A s I pen down these final words, "I forgive you," they carry the weight of every tear you have shed, every moment of your pain endured, and every breath you have taken amidst the struggle to find peace. These words are not just a statement; they are a testament to the journey of healing, a declaration of freedom from the chains of hurt and pain that have held so many captives for far too long.

Forgiveness is not a sign of weakness, nor is it an easy path to walk. It requires immense strength, courage, and an unwavering commitment to personal growth and healing. It means confronting the darkest moments with the light of empathy and understanding. It means choosing to release the bitterness and anger that may have taken root in your hearts, not for the sake of those who have wronged you, but for your personal well-being and peace.

To forgive is to acknowledge the hurt and pain but refuse to let it define or control your life. It is to understand that while we cannot change the past, we hold the power to shape our future. It is an act of reclaiming our narrative, of writing our story with words of hope, resilience, and compassion.

"I Forgive You: Choosing Forgiveness Over Bondage" is not just about the other person; it is about us. It is about healing the wounds, mending the broken pieces, and emerging stronger and more whole than before. It is about recognizing your worth and affirming that no amount of hurt can diminish your value.

As you utter these words, "I forgive you," let them be a balm to your soul, a gentle reminder that you are not alone in this journey. There is a world of support and understanding waiting to embrace you, to walk with you as you navigate the path of forgiveness. Let these words be a beacon of hope, illuminating the way forward, and guiding you towards a future filled with peace, joy, and endless possibilities.

"I Forgive You: Choosing Forgiveness Over Bondage" is an invitation to let go of the past, embrace the present, and step confidently into the future. It is a courageous choice to love yourself enough to move beyond the hurt and to open your heart to a life unburdened by unforgiveness. As you stand at the crossroads of hurt and healing, may you find the strength to take the step towards forgiveness, knowing that in doing so, you are embarking on a remarkable journey of transformation and liberation.

With heartfelt compassion and a genuine wish for your healing and happiness,

Dr. Donna D. Ferguson

APPENDIX

APPENDIX

EXAMPLE LETTERS FOR FORGIVENESS

riting a letter can be a therapeutic exercise in the process of dealing with unforgiveness, helping to articulate feelings and thoughts that may be difficult to express. Here are a few example letters written from the perspective of someone dealing with unforgiveness, along with instructions for how to approach this exercise. It's important to remember that these letters are for the writer's healing and it's not necessary to send them to the one that hurt you unless it feels appropriate and safe to do so. If you are in treatment, never send a letter without processing it through with your therapist.

INSTRUCTIONS FOR WRITING THE LETTER:

1. **Find a Quiet Space**: Choose a quiet and comfortable place where you can be alone with your thoughts.
2. **Allow Yourself to Feel**: As you write, allow yourself to feel whatever emotions arise. Don't censor yourself; this letter is just for you unless you decide otherwise.
3. **Be Honest and Direct**: Express all that you have been holding back. This might include hurt, anger, disappointment, or confusion.
4. **Take Your Time**: Don't rush through the process. You might find it takes several attempts or sessions to say all you want to say.
5. **Closure**: Once you've finished, you can choose what to do with the letter. Some people find it helpful to keep it, others prefer to destroy it as a symbolic release of the pain.

Example Letter (Broad):

Dear [Name],

I've been carrying this weight for a long time, and I need to release it for my own sake. You hurt me deeply when [describe the situation], and it has been affecting me in ways I didn't fully realize until now. I've felt angry, betrayed, and saddened by what happened.

I've wondered many times how you could have [describe the action or behavior], how you didn't see the pain it would cause. These questions have haunted me, disrupting my peace and happiness. As I write this, I'm trying to understand, not to excuse what happened, but to find a path to forgiveness for my own well-being.

I'm learning that forgiving you is really about healing myself. It's about deciding that I no longer want to carry this burden of resentment and anger. It doesn't mean forgetting or saying what happened was acceptable. It's about letting go of the hold this pain has over me.

I don't know if I'm there yet, but I am trying. This letter is a step for me, a way to express all the hurt and start moving beyond it. You may never read these words, but I needed to write them for me. I forgive you.

Sincerely,
[Your Name]

Example Letter (Broad):

Dear [Name],

For a long time, I've been silent about how deeply your actions hurt me. Holding onto this silence seemed easier than facing the pain head-on. But now, I realize it's been festering, turning into bitterness and resentment that's been hard to shake off.

You might not have been aware, but when you [describe the incident or behavior], it left a significant mark on me. It's been challenging to see past the hurt, to understand why it happened, and how I can move forward.

This letter is part of my journey towards healing. It's important for me to acknowledge the pain, to say it out loud, even if only on paper. I am trying to work through these feelings of shame, blame, and embarrassment to name a few. I'm trying to understand and to let go, I desire to forgive you.

Forgiveness is for me, not for you. It's about my freedom, my emotional and mental well-being. It's a process, one that I am taking one day at a time. This letter is a step in that process, a way for me to confront what happened and articulate the impact it has had on me.

I am doing this for me, to close this chapter and move on to a healthier, happier life. Whether or not this letter reaches you, know that it is a part of my path to letting go and healing. I forgive you.

Sincerely,
[Your Name]

CLOSING NOTE FOR THE WRITER:

Remember, this letter is for you. It's a step towards healing and finding peace. Once you have written it, you decide what to do next. You can keep it in a safe place, destroy it, or if it feels right, and only if it feels safe and appropriate, consider sending it. The most important thing is that this letter serves your journey towards forgiveness and healing.

EXAMPLE LETTER FOR FORGIVING PARENTS

Here are two example letters from an adult child to a parent addressing hurtful experiences from childhood. Again, this letter is intended as a therapeutic exercise for the writer and may not be suitable for sending depending on individual circumstances and the current nature of the relationship.

Example Letter:

Dear [Parent's Name],

I've been carrying some heavy feelings for a long time, and I need to release them to heal and move forward. It's taken me years to find the courage to express how your words and actions during my childhood affected me. This letter isn't meant to blame, but rather to shed light on my feelings and experiences in hopes of finding some peace.

You might not have been aware of the impact of you're your words and actions or perhaps the circumstances were beyond your control, but as a child, I felt [describe feelings - neglected, unloved, hurt, etc.]. When you [specific behavior or incident], it left a deep mark on me.

These experiences shaped how I view myself and the world around me. I've struggled with [mention any repercussions like trust issues, low self-esteem, etc.], and it's been a challenging journey to understand and work through these feelings.

I am writing this letter as part of my healing process. I've learned that harboring resentment and anger only holds me back. Forgiving you is not about condoning what happened; it's about freeing myself from the bitterness and pain that have lingered for years. It's about healing the child within me and allowing myself to live fully in the present.

This journey of forgiveness is mine, and it's not dependent on your response or even an apology, though any acknowledgment of the past would be meaningful. It's about me reclaiming my story and finding peace. I am learning to let go of what I cannot change and focus on building a healthier and happier life for myself and my future.

Despite everything, I wish to understand and empathize with your struggles and experiences that might have contributed to those hurtful times. We all have our journeys, and perhaps this letter might open a path for a better understanding between us.

Please know that I am working towards forgiveness for both of our sakes. It's a process, one that takes time, but I am committed to it. I hope one day we can find a new way to relate to each other, one that is based on mutual respect and understanding. Just know that I forgive you.

With hope for the future,
[Your Name]

This letter is a deeply personal reflection and a step toward healing. Sending a letter to a parent can be somewhat overwhelming as it is a form of confronting, which is often difficult whether you send the letter or not. Whether or not you choose to send it is entirely up to you and should be based on what will best serve your emotional well-being and the nature of your current relationship with your parent. Remember, the primary goal is your healing and finding a path toward peace and understanding.

FORGIVING PARENTS

Forgiving parents, especially for hurts stemming from childhood, can be one of the most challenging forms of forgiveness. The parent-child relationship is foundational; it significantly influences one's emotional development, sense of security, and understanding of love and trust. When this relationship is tainted by hurt, neglect, or abuse, the wounds can run exceptionally deep, making forgiveness a complex and often painful process.

THE CHALLENGE OF FORGIVING PARENTS

1. **Shattered Trust and Safety**: Parents are typically a child's first source of love, safety, and trust. When parents inflict hurt or fail to protect, it doesn't just cause immediate pain; it disrupts the fundamental trust and safety a child should feel. The betrayal is profound because it comes from the very individuals who are biologically and socially programmed to care and nurture.

2. **Long-Term Emotional Impact**: The effects of childhood hurt often extend far into adulthood, influencing one's self-esteem,

forming relationships, and overall mental health. The deep-seated nature of these wounds makes the process of revisiting and forgiving these hurts incredibly challenging.

3. **Complex Family Dynamics**: Family relationships and loyalties can complicate feelings of unforgiveness towards parents. There may be pressure to maintain family harmony or conflicting feelings of love and resentment towards the parent. The desire to protect the family image or not to cause further conflict can hinder the process of addressing and forgiving past hurts.

4. **Repeated or Unacknowledged Hurt**: Sometimes, the hurt from parents is not a single event but a pattern of behavior over the years. If the hurtful behavior continues into adulthood or if the parents do not acknowledge the pain they've caused, it can make forgiving them even more challenging.

THE IMPORTANCE OF FORGIVING PARENTS

1. **Emotional Freedom and Healing**: Forgiving parents is often a crucial step in healing from childhood wounds. It allows individuals to release the hold that past hurts have on their emotional well-being. This doesn't mean excusing the parents or forgetting what happened, but rather processing the emotions and finding peace.

2. **Breaking the Cycle**: By working through forgiveness, individuals can break the cycle of hurt and prevent the perpetuation of negative patterns in their own lives and relationships. It's an opportunity to learn from the past and make conscious choices about the future.

3. **Improved Mental and Physical Health**: Holding onto anger and resentment towards parents can lead to chronic stress and associated health problems. Forgiveness has been linked to

better mental and physical health, including reduced anxiety, depression, and symptoms of chronic illness.

4. **Reconstructing Relationships**: For some, forgiving parents can open the door to rebuilding or redefining the relationship. It might lead to a more honest dialogue about the past and an opportunity to establish new boundaries and healthier interactions.

5. **Personal Growth and Maturity**: Forgiving parents often requires a deep level of personal growth and emotional maturity. It involves empathy, understanding, and a broader perspective on human relationships and fallibility. This growth can enrich all areas of life, leading to more profound relationships and a greater sense of personal peace.

Forgiving parents is undoubtedly a complex and deeply personal journey. It requires courage, time, and often, guidance from supportive friends, family, or a professional therapist. While it's a challenging process, the potential benefits to one's emotional health, relationships, and overall quality of life make it a journey worth undertaking for many individuals. Each step taken towards forgiveness is a step towards healing, not just from past hurts, but also towards a more compassionate and understanding view of oneself and others.

EXAMPLE LETTER OF ENGAGEMENT BROKEN

Here's an example letter written from the perspective of someone who was engaged, but their partner called off the wedding, leaving them with feelings of unforgiveness, shame, and embarrassment. This letter is a personal exercise for healing and isn't necessarily meant to be sent.

Example Letter:

Dear [Ex-Partner's Name],

It has taken me a long time to find the words to express what has been swirling inside me since the day our paths separated. When you decided to call off our wedding, it wasn't just the end of our relationship; it felt like the crumbling of all the dreams and plans we had built together. The shock and pain were profound, and in many ways, they still linger.

I've felt a wide range of emotions since that day - disbelief, anger, deep sadness, and an overwhelming sense of shame and embarrassment. I've questioned my worth, our love, and the very foundation of what I believed our relationship was. The public nature of our planned commitment turned into a public spectacle of its withdrawal, leaving me to navigate not only my own feelings of loss but also the perceived judgment and pity of others.

This letter is for me, a step toward healing and releasing the bitterness and hurt that I've been carrying. I'm learning that holding onto these feelings only ties me more closely to the most painful moments of my life. Forgiving you is one of the most challenging things I am trying to do, but I know it's necessary for me to move on and reclaim my happiness and peace.

Forgiving you doesn't mean I understand or condone what happened. It doesn't erase the hurt or the public humiliation I've felt. But it does mean that I'm choosing to let go of the hold these feelings have on me. I'm choosing to not let this experience define me or dictate my future happiness.

I'm working to understand that everyone has their own struggles and reasons, and while I may never fully understand why you did what you did, I am trying to accept it as part of my past. I'm also working to forgive myself for any perceived failings I've dwelled on or the embarrassment I've felt.

I don't know what the future holds for either of us, but I do know that I want to move forward with grace and strength. I hope that in time, the pain will continue to fade, replaced by new experiences and learnings that will shape me into a more resilient and compassionate person.

I am striving to find closure, not from your words or actions, but from my own inner work and the support of those who love me. This letter marks a step in that journey, a journey towards healing, forgiveness, and a future where the weight of this pain no longer holds me back. So as a result, I choose to forgive you.

Sincerely,
[Your Name]

CLOSING NOTE FOR THE WRITER:

This letter is a personal reflection meant to articulate and process your feelings. Whether or not you decide to send it, the act of writing it is a powerful step in your healing journey. It's about expressing your emotions, not about eliciting a response or change from the other person. Remember, forgiveness is for you - a path to release the burden of hurt and reclaim your inner peace.

EXAMPLE LETTER OF BEING HURT BY CHURCH LEADERSHIP

Here's an example of a letter from someone who has been hurt by their church leadership and congregation. This letter is a personal expression meant to aid in the healing process of the individual and is not necessarily intended for sending.

Example Letter:

Dear [Church/Leader's Name],

I am writing this letter with a heavy heart and a conflicted mind. The church, which was once a sanctuary for me, a place of peace and community, became a source of deep hurt and disillusionment. The events and actions, or perhaps inactions, of the leadership and congregation, have left me feeling betrayed, marginalized, and deeply wounded.

My faith has always been a cornerstone of my life, guiding me through good times and bad. It was within the church's walls that I sought solace, community, and spiritual growth. However, when [describe the situation or incident], it not only shook my trust in the individuals involved but in the institution that I had held in such high regard.

The hurt I feel is not just about the incident itself, but about the response - or lack thereof - from those I looked up to and respected. The feeling of being judged, misunderstood, or ignored by my spiritual family added layers of pain and confusion. It has been challenging to reconcile the messages of love, forgiveness, and community that are preached from the pulpit with the reality of my experience.

This letter is a step in my journey toward healing. I am trying to unpack and understand the multitude of emotions that I have been carrying - anger, sadness, loss of faith, and a profound sense of betrayal. I am learning that holding onto these feelings of unforgiveness is hindering my spiritual and emotional well-being. It is not easy, but I am striving to forgive, not for the sake of anyone else, but for my own peace and liberation.

Forgiving does not mean forgetting, nor does it negate the validity of my feelings or the wrongness of what happened. It is about releasing the grip that this hurt has on my heart and mind. It is about choosing to not let this experience define my relationship with faith, God, or community.

As I write this, I am still navigating my feelings towards the church and what my future within it might look like. I am seeking a path forward that allows me to retain my faith while also protecting my heart and spirit. I hope that in time, I will find a way to reconnect with a spiritual community that embodies the true principles of love, acceptance, and forgiveness that I value so deeply. Today, I choose to forgive you.

This journey is mine to walk, and this letter is a step along that path. Thank you for being a part of my story, even if it's not in the way I had hoped or expected. I pray that my experience will serve as a catalyst for reflection and positive change within the church, fostering an environment where all feel truly welcome and supported.

With a hopeful heart,
[Your Name]

CLOSING NOTE FOR THE WRITER:

This letter is a personal reflection, a means to articulate and process the complex emotions you're experiencing. It is not uncommon for someone to lose faith and fail to trust God, sometimes walk away from God because of the hurt they experienced in the church. This is one of the most painful journeys through forgiveness because those who suffer from the church gave all of themselves and could not imagine being hurt. Whether you choose to send this letter, keep it, or destroy it after writing, the most important aspect is that it serves your journey of healing and forgiveness. Remember, you're not alone in feeling hurt by a place that was supposed to be safe and nurturing. Your path to healing is valid and important.

EXAMPLE LETTERS:

Letter to a Business Partner Who Cheated You

Dear [Business Partner's Name],

I am writing this letter after much reflection on the events that have transpired between us. When we entered our partnership, I did so with trust and optimism, believing in our shared vision and integrity. Discovering that you cheated me in our business dealings was not only a financial blow but a deep personal betrayal. It has taken me some time to process the hurt and the breach of trust.

However, I am choosing to write to you today from a place of forgiveness. This decision is not an approval of your actions, nor does it erase the consequences. Instead, it is an act of self-liberation. Holding onto anger and resentment serves no one, least of all me.

I am forgiving you to free myself from the bitterness that has been weighing me down and to move forward with my life and career with a clear conscience and heart.

Sincerely,
[Your Name]

Letter to a Friend Who Mishandled You

Dear [Friend's Name],

We have shared so many memories and experiences, and it's with a heavy heart that I address the way you mishandled and mistreated me. Your actions deeply hurt me, and it felt like a betrayal of the friendship we built. I have spent considerable time hurt and confused by what happened.

Today, I am writing to let you know that I am working on forgiving you. This is not about condoning what you did or pretending everything is okay between us. It's about my own healing. It's about not carrying the weight of hurt and disappointment any longer. I hope you understand the impact of your actions and learn from this situation as I have and because it's my choice, I forgive you.

Warm regards,
[Your Name]

Letter to Someone Who Bullied You

Dear [Bully's Name],

For a long time, your words and actions cast a shadow over my life. Being bullied by you left deep scars and affected how I viewed myself and interacted with the world. The fear and pain I experienced were real and long-lasting. It's taken me a lot of courage and strength to reach a place where I can address this.

I am writing to inform you that I am choosing to forgive you. This is not for your sake but for mine. Forgiving you means I am no longer holding onto the pain and letting it define me. I am doing this so I can live freely, without the anger and resentment that were holding me back.

Best,
[Your Name]

Letter to Someone Who Used You

Dear [Person's Name],

When I realized the extent to which you used me for your own benefit, it was a profound shock and disappointment. Trust is not easily given, and to see mine exploited affected me deeply. The journey to understanding and processing this has been long and challenging.

I have decided to forgive you, not because what you did was acceptable, but because I deserve peace. This forgiveness is a step towards healing my own heart and reclaiming my power. I hope you reflect on your actions and their impact on others.

Sincerely,
[Your Name]

Letter to Someone Who Stole from You

Dear [Person's Name],

The discovery that you stole from me was not just a loss of possessions but a breach of trust. Such actions have consequences, not only materially but emotionally and relationally. The disappointment and violation I felt were overwhelming.

However, I am choosing to forgive you. This decision is about liberating myself from the anger and desire for retribution. I hope that you will understand the gravity of your actions and make amends in whatever way possible. Forgiving you is my way of closing this painful chapter and moving forward with my life.

Regards,
[Your Name]

Letter to Someone Who Embarrassed You

Dear [Person's Name],

The embarrassment and humiliation I felt from your actions have lingered in my mind longer than I'd like to admit. Being demeaned, especially in a public setting, was a deeply unsettling experience that affected my self-esteem and confidence.

I've decided to write this letter as part of my journey to forgive you. This isn't about forgetting what happened or diminishing its impact. Instead, it's about not letting that moment define me or our interaction forever. Forgiveness is my path to overcoming the hurt and reclaiming my dignity and because it is my journey, I choose to forgive you.

Yours,
[Your Name]

EXAMPLE OF LETTERS OF BETRAYAL, INFIDELITY, RACIAL DISCRIMINATION, SEXUAL ASSAULT, AND DOMESTIC VIOLENCE

When writing letters of forgiveness for different forms of hurt such as betrayal, infidelity, racial discrimination, sexual assault, and domestic violence, it's essential to approach each subject with sensitivity, empathy, and understanding of the profound emotional impact these experiences can have. Remember: Each of these letters is deeply personal and reflects a journey towards healing and reclaiming power.

Forgiveness Letter for Betrayal

Dear [Name],

As I write this letter, a whirlwind of emotions courses through me, the most prominent being pain and disbelief from the betrayal I experienced. You were someone I trusted and valued in my life, and discovering your betrayal felt like the ground was swept from beneath me.

Despite the hurt and the chaos that followed, I am writing to you today to express my journey towards forgiveness. This does not excuse or diminish the gravity of your actions but rather marks a decision I've made for my peace and healing. Forgiving you is not about erasing the past but about releasing the heavy burden of anger and resentment that I've carried.

It's been a challenging journey, filled with introspection and a deep desire to understand why. While I may never fully grasp the reasons behind your actions, I've come to realize that holding onto my hurt only ties me to the pain. Forgiving you means freeing myself from this tie, allowing me to move forward with hope and strength. Today, I choose to forgive you.

Sincerely,
[Your Name]

Forgiveness Letter for Infidelity

Dear [Name],

The revelation of your infidelity was a moment that changed the trajectory of my life. It shattered my trust and broke the sanctity of our relationship. The hurt and betrayal I felt were overwhelming, and for a long time, it consumed my thoughts and tainted my view of love and trust.

Today, I am writing to you not to forget or excuse what happened but to let you know that I am working on forgiving you. This forgiveness is for me - a step towards healing and reclaiming the joy and peace I deserve. It's a journey that's required every ounce of strength and courage I have, and while it's far from over, it's a path I choose to take.

Please know that this forgiveness does not mean reconciliation or a restoration of our relationship. It means that I am choosing not to let your actions define my happiness or my future. It's about me moving forward, with or without you, with a lighter heart and a clearer mind.

With a hopeful heart,
[Your Name]

Forgiveness Letter for Racial Discrimination

Dear [Name or Institution],

Experiencing racial discrimination at your hands was not just an incident; it was a painful reminder of the injustices that continue to permeate our society. The hurt and anger it invoked were profound, touching the very core of my identity and dignity.

I am writing this letter as a testament to my resilience and as a step towards healing. Forgiving you is one of the most challenging decisions I've made, driven not by acceptance of what happened, but by a commitment to rise above it. This forgiveness is an act of empowerment, a declaration that your actions will not define me or diminish my worth.

This journey is not a removal of the hurt or the reality of racism but a personal reclaiming of power and peace. It's about transforming my pain into a catalyst for change and growth, both personally and within my community. Today, I forgive you.

In pursuit of justice and equality,
[Your Name]

Forgiveness Letter for Sexual Assault

Dear [Name],

Writing this letter is perhaps one of the most difficult things I've done, as it forces me to confront the deep and lasting pain caused by the sexual assault you inflicted upon me. The experience left scars that are not visible but have impacted every aspect of my life.

Forgiving you is not about forgetting or minimizing the gravity of your actions. It is about my healing, my decision to not let this assault define my future, or my sense of self. It is an incredibly personal journey, filled with anger, sadness, and eventually, a tough, resilient hope.

This letter does not mean that I am okay with what happened or that justice shouldn't be served. It means that I am choosing to release the hold that this trauma has on my heart and mind. It's a step towards living a life not overshadowed by the pain you caused.

With a resilient spirit, I sincerely forgive you

[Your Name]

Forgiveness Letter for Domestic Violence

Dear [Name],

The time I spent under the shadow of domestic violence was a period of constant fear, pain, and degradation. The physical and emotional wounds you inflicted upon me were acts that I once thought I could never move past or forgive.

I am writing this letter to acknowledge the difficult journey I've been on toward healing and forgiveness. This forgiveness does not, in any way, condone or diminish the severity of your actions. Rather, it's about liberating myself from the cycle of pain and anger that bound me to those dark moments.

I've learned that forgiveness is a path to regaining my strength and dignity. It's not about you; it's about me and my journey towards a future of peace and self-empowerment. I am reclaiming my life, one step at a time, and this letter is a significant step in that journey. Despite being able to recall it all, I choose to forgive you.

In pursuit of peace and healing,
[Your Name]

Each of these letters is deeply personal and reflects a complex journey of emotions, thoughts, and decisions. Writing such a letter is a personal choice and one that should be made with careful consideration and, if necessary, with the support of trusted friends, family, or a professional therapist. The journey towards forgiveness is unique to each individual and situation, and these letters are merely examples to inspire and guide those who wish to express their feelings and thoughts on their path to healing.

REFERENCES

Larsen, Britta A., Ryan S. Darby, Christine R. Harris, Dana Kay Nelkin, Per-Erik Milam, and Nicholas J.S. Christenfeld. "The Immediate and Delayed Cardiovascular Benefits of Forgiving." *Psychosomatic Medicine* 74, no. 7 (2012): 745-750. Accessed 2024. doi: 10.1097/ psy.0b013e31825fe96c.

Toussaint, Loren L., Everett L. Worthington, and David R. Williams. "Introduction: Context, Overview, and Guiding Questions." *Forgiveness and Health* (2015): 1-9. Accessed 2024. doi: 10.1007/978-94-017-9993- 5_1

Wade, Nathaniel G., William T. Hoyt, Julia E. M. Kidwell, and Everett L. Worthington. "Efficacy of Psychotherapeutic Interventions to Promote Forgiveness: A Meta-Analysis." *Journal of Consulting and Clinical Psychology* 82, no. 1 (2014): 154-170. Accessed 2024. doi: 10.1037/ a0035268.

Jr., Everett Worthington,. *Moving Forward: Six steps to forgiving yourself and breaking free from the past.* WaterBrook, 2013.

TERMINOLOGY

1. **Anger:** A strong feeling of annoyance, displeasure, or hostility.
2. **Behavior:** The way in which one acts or conducts oneself, especially towards others.
3. **Betrayal:** The act of betraying someone or something, or the fact of being betrayed; violation of a person's trust or confidence.
4. **Bitterness:** Long-lasting resentment or deep-seated ill will.
5. **Cognition:** The mental action or process of acquiring knowledge and understanding through thought, experience, and the senses.
6. **Compassion:** A deep awareness of the suffering of another coupled with the wish to relieve it. It involves empathy and a desire to help or be kind to others.
7. **Culture:** The social behavior and norms found in human societies as well as the knowledge, beliefs, arts, laws, customs, capabilities, and habits of the individuals in these groups.
8. **Emotion:** A complex reaction pattern, involving experiential, behavioral, and physiological elements, by which an individual attempts to deal with a personally significant matter or event.
9. **Emotional Encoding:** The process of converting a particularly vivid or emotionally charged experience into a memory that is stored and recalled.
10. **Emotional Scarring:** Long-lasting effects and inner wounds that occur as a result of prolonged or intense emotional trauma or distress.

11. **Empowerment:** The process of becoming stronger and more confident, especially in controlling one's life and claiming one's rights.

12. **Fear:** An unpleasant emotion caused by the belief that someone or something is dangerous, likely to cause pain, or a threat.

13. **Forgiveness:** The act of pardoning someone for an offense or mistake they've made. It often requires a conscious decision to let go of resentment and thoughts of revenge.

14. **Hostility:** Hostile behavior; unfriendliness or opposition.

15. **Identity:** The qualities, beliefs, personality, looks and/or expressions that make a person or group.

16. **Meditation:** A practice where an individual uses a technique – such as mindfulness, or focusing the mind on a particular object, thought, or activity – to train attention and awareness, and achieve a mentally clear and emotionally calm and stable state.

17. **Memory:** The faculty by which the mind stores and remembers information.

18. **Mindfulness:** A mental state achieved by focusing one's awareness on the present moment, while calmly acknowledging and accepting one's feelings, thoughts, and bodily sensations, often used as a therapeutic technique.

19. **Morals:** Principles or habits with respect to right or wrong conduct. They guide individuals in judging what is right and wrong, often informed by cultural, religious, or philosophical values.

20. **Optimism:** Hopefulness and confidence about the future or the successful outcome of something.

21. **Personal Growth:** The process of improving oneself through such activities as enhancing talents, increasing consciousness and self-awareness, and building wealth or social status.

22. **Rage:** Violent and uncontrolled anger.

23. **Reconciliation:** The process of restoring friendly relations between individuals or groups after conflict or disagreement. It involves mutual acceptance, forgiveness, and a commitment to move forward positively.

24. **Religious Trauma:** The experience of severe psychological harm caused by an individual's involvement with or exposure to religious beliefs, practices, or structures.

25. **Remorse:** A deep regret or guilt for a wrong committed. It involves recognizing one's actions have caused harm and feeling genuinely sorry about the consequences.

26. **Repressed Memory:** A memory that has been unconsciously blocked due to the memory being associated with a high level of stress or trauma.

27. **Resentment:** is a complex, deeply felt form of anger and displeasure stemming from a sense of being wronged or treated unfairly. It often arises in response to perceived injustice, betrayal, or hurt. Characteristics of resentment include *Duration:* Resentment can linger long after the offending action took place, sometimes lasting for years. *Bitterness:* It carries a persistent bitterness and emotional rehearsing of the hurtful event. *Blame:* There is often a focus on blaming the other person or situation for one's own pain and suffering. Reluctance to Forgive: Resentment is closely tied to an unwillingness or inability to forgive the perceived offense. It's noteworthy to say that its impact on Relationships can be significant, leading to hostility, communication breakdown, and a desire for retribution or justice. Resentment can be corrosive, affecting individuals' well-being, relationships, and overall outlook on life. *It often requires conscious effort and sometimes professional help to resolve and move beyond.*

28. **Responsibility:** The state or fact of having a duty to deal with something or of having control over someone. It often involves being accountable for one's actions or decisions.

29. **Resentment:** Bitter indignation at having been treated unfairly.

30. **Self-Compassion:** is a positive, caring attitude towards oneself in the face of personal failings, inadequacies, or suffering. It involves three main components: *Self-kindness*: Being gentle and understanding with oneself rather than harshly critical or judgmental. *Common humanity*: Recognizing that suffering and personal failure are part of the shared human experience – something that everyone goes through rather than being something that happens to "me" alone. *Mindfulness*: Holding one's painful thoughts and feelings in balanced awareness rather than over-identifying with them. Self-compassion allows individuals to acknowledge and accept their mistakes and flaws with kindness and understanding, enabling them to learn and grow from experiences rather than being overwhelmed by negative self-judgment.

31. **Self-Reflection:** The activity of thinking about your own feelings and behavior, and the reasons that may lie behind them.

32. **Self-Worth:** The sense of one's own value or worth as a person; self- esteem; self-respect.

33. **Spiritual distress**: A disturbance in a person's belief or value system. It may occur when a person is unable to find sources of meaning, hope, love, peace, comfort, strength, and connection in life or when conflict occurs between his/her beliefs and what is happening in their life.

34. **Stress:** The body's reaction to any change that requires an adjustment or response. It can be physical, mental, or emotional and is often caused by good or bad experiences.

35. **Suppressed Memory:** Intentionally or unintentionally hindering the recall of a memory, often because it is too disturbing or traumatic to remember.

36. **Thought:** An idea or opinion produced by thinking or occurring suddenly in the mind.

37. **Values:** Core beliefs or standards that guide an individual's behavior and decision-making. Values reflect what is important to the individual and often influence their goals and ways of living.

Contact US

 833.818.5550

 Info@dfsoulutions.com

 www.DFSoulutions.com

DF SOULUTIONS

TRANSFORMING LIVES ONE MIND AT A TIME

CONCISE PUBLISHING

SELF PUBLISHING MADE
EASY

Let Us Be Your

ONE STOP
SHOP

Ghost Writing   Formatting
Editing   Cover Design
eBook Creation   Distribution
              & More

Email Us @ info@ConcisePublishing.us

THE KING and His GLORY (PART 2)
MORE GOLD FROM THE BOOK OF ISAIAH ABOUT THE COMING KING OF GLORY

GREG HARRIS

Never stop Dreaming
IT WILL WORK THIS TIME

30 DAY DEVOTIONAL
LET GO OF THE COOKIES
Do You See What They See In You?
James Edwards

THE LIE
and other BIBLICAL TRUTHS from the COMING TRIBULATION
Greg Harris

DELIVERANCE FOR REAL
Dr. Shirley R. Brown, Th.D
WORKBOOK

TEMEILA C. DANIEL

A Guide to Virtual Meeting
NETIQUETTE

GEORGE BLOOMER SCHOOL OF MINISTRY PRESENTS
Warfarecology
ALTARS & UNGODLY COVENANTS
BISHOP GEORGE BLOOMER

SOD
SECRETS OF DELIVERANCE
The Bishop's Notes
GEORGE BLOOMER
BEST SELLING AUTHOR OF WITCHCRAFT IN THE PEWS

Miss Carter's HANDWRITING
PRACTICE YOUR ABC's AND COLORING BOOK
DOLLETTE CARTER

Made in the USA
Las Vegas, NV
02 August 2024

93306301R00085